LEADER'S GUIDE

Dr. Van Bogard Dunn, writer of this study resource, is Professor Emeritus and Dean Emeritus at the Methodist Theological School in Ohio. He is a graduate of Murray State University and Duke Divinity School. In his long career as a professor and student of the New Testament, Dr. Dunn has shared his knowledge with the general church, writing for both Church School Publications and Discipleship Resources. "Bogie," as students lovingly call him, is married to the former Geraldine Hurt. They have four children and seven grandchildren. In retirement, "Bogie" continues to share his love for the Scripture with the church. He also is a talented cabinetmaker, specializing in creating reproduction Shaker furniture.

JOURNEY THROUGH THE BIBLE: MATTHEW. LEADER'S GUIDE. An official resource for The United Methodist Church prepared by the General Board of Discipleship through the division of Church School Publications and published by Cokesbury, a division of The United Methodist Publishing House; 201 Eighth Avenue, South; P. O. Box 801; Nashville, TN 37202. Printed in the United States of America.

Scripture quotations in this publication, unless otherwise indicated, are from the New Revised Standard Version of the Bible, copyright © by the Division of Christian Education of the National Council of the churches of Christ in the United States of America, and are used by permission. All rights reserved.

For permission to reproduce any material in this publication, call 1-615-749-6421, or write to Cokesbury, Syndication–Permissions Office, 201 Eighth Avenue, South, P.O. Box 801, Nashville, TN 37202.

To order copies of this publication, call toll free 1-800-672-1789. Call Monday–Friday 7:30-5:00 Central Time or 8:30-4:30 Pacific Time. Use your Cokesbury account, American Express, Visa, Discover, or MasterCard.

© Copyright 1994. All rights reserved.

 Cokesbury

EDITORIAL TEAM

Debra G. Ball-Kilbourne,
Editor

Linda H. Leach,
Assistant Editor

Linda O. Spicer,
Adult Department Assistant

DESIGN TEAM

Susan J. Scruggs,
Design Supervisor,
Cover Design

Ed Wynne,
Layout Designer

ADMINISTRATIVE STAFF

Duane A. Ewers,
Editor of Church School Publications

Dal Joon Won,
Managing Editor of Church School Publications

Gary L. Ball-Kilbourne,
Executive Editor of Adult Publications

THIS PUBLICATION IS PRINTED ON RECYCLED PAPER

CONTENTS

Volume 9: Matthew — by Van Bogard Dunn

Introduction		2
Chapter 1	THE BIRTH OF JESUS THE MESSIAH: EMMANUEL	3
Chapter 2	THE BAPTISM AND TEMPTATION OF JESUS THE MESSIAH: SON OF GOD	8
Chapter 3	THE MINISTRY OF JESUS THE MESSIAH: PREACHING	13
Chapter 4	THE MINISTRY OF JESUS THE MESSIAH: TEACHING	18
Chapter 5	THE MINISTRY OF JESUS THE MESSIAH: HEALING	23
Chapter 6	THE MINISTRY OF JESUS THE MESSIAH ACCEPTED: AUTHORITY TO PREACH AND HEAL	28
Chapter 7	THE MINISTRY OF JESUS THE MESSIAH REJECTED: BLASPHEMY AGAINST THE HOLY SPIRIT	33
Chapter 8	THE MINISTRY OF JESUS THE MESSIAH MISUNDERSTOOD: THE NECESSITY OF THE CROSS	38
Chapter 9	THE MINISTRY OF JESUS THE MESSIAH DENIED: THE GRIEF OF SELF-RELIANCE	43
Chapter 10	THE MINISTRY OF JESUS THE MESSIAH AFFIRMED: THE PRAISE OF BABIES	48
Chapter 11	THE MINISTRY OF JESUS THE MESSIAH NOW AND NOT YET: THE COMING JUDGMENT	53
Chapter 12	THE MINISTRY OF JESUS THE MESSIAH COMPLETED: AGONY AND TRIUMPH	58
Chapter 13	THE MINISTRY OF JESUS THE MESSIAH CONTINUED: COMMISSION AND PROMISE	63
HOW TO CREATE EXCITEMENT FOR BIBLE STUDY		68
MATTHEW AND HIS GOSPEL		70
MAP OF PALESTINE IN JESUS' TIME		Inside back cover

INTRODUCTION

The leader's guides provided for use with JOURNEY THROUGH THE BIBLE make the following assumptions:
- adults learn in different ways:
  - by reading
  - by listening to speakers
  - by working on projects
  - by drama and roleplay
  - by using their imaginations
  - by expressing themselves creatively
  - by teaching others
- the mix of persons in your group is different from that found in any other group.
- the length of the actual time you have for teaching in a session may vary from thirty minutes to ninety minutes.
- the physical place where your class meets is not exactly like the place where any other group or class meets.
- your teaching skills, experiences, and preferences are unlike anyone else's.

We encourage you to discover and develop the ways you can best use the information and learning ideas in this leader's guide with your particular class. To get started, we suggest you try following these steps:

1. Think and pray about your individual class members. Who are they? What are they like? Why are they involved in this particular Bible study class at this particular time in their lives? What seem to be their needs? How do you think they learn best?
2. Think and pray about your class members as a group. A group takes on a character that can be different from the particular characters of the individuals who make up that group. How do your class members interact? What do they enjoy doing together? What would help them become stronger as a group?
3. Keep in mind that you are teaching this class for the sake of the class members, in order to help them increase in their faithfulness as disciples of Jesus Christ. Teachers sometimes fall prey to the danger of teaching in ways that are easiest for themselves. The best teachers accept the discomfort of taking risks and stretching their teaching skills in order to focus on what will really help the class members learn and grow in their faith.
4. Read the chapter in the study book. Read the assigned Bible passages. Read the background Bible passages, if any. Work through the Dimension 1 questions in the study book. Make a list of any items you do not understand and need to research further using such tools as Bible dictionaries, concordances, Bible atlases, and commentaries. In other words, do your homework. Be prepared with your own knowledge about the Bible passages being studied by your class.
5. Read the chapter's material in the leader's guide. You might want to begin with the "Additional Bible Helps," found at the *end* of each chapter in the leader's guide. Then look at each learning idea in the "Learning Menu."
6. Spend some time with the "Learning Menu." Notice that the "Learning Menu" is organized around Dimensions 1, 2, and 3 in the study book. Recognizing that different adults and adult classes will learn best using different teaching/learning methods, in each of the three dimensions you will find
   - at least one learning idea that is primarily discussion-based;
   - at least one learning idea that begins with a method other than discussion, but which may lead into discussion.

   Make notes about which learning ideas will work best given the unique makeup and setting of your class.
7. Decide on a lesson plan: Which learning ideas will you lead the class members through when? What materials will you need? What other preparations do you need to make? How long do you plan to spend on a particular learning idea?
8. Many experienced teachers have found that they do better if they plan more than they actually use during a class session. They also know that their class members may become frustrated if they try to do too much during a class session. In other words
   - plan more than you can actually use. That way, you have back-up learning ideas in case something does not work well or something takes much less time than you thought.
   - don't try to do everything listed in the "Learning Menu." We have intentionally offered you much more than you can use in one class session.
   - be flexible while you teach. A good lesson plan is only a guide for your use as you teach people. Keep the focus on your class members, not your lesson plan.
9. After you teach, evaluate the class session. What worked well? What did not? What did you learn from your experience of teaching that will help you plan for the next class session?

May God's Spirit be upon you as you lead your class on their *Journey Through the Bible*!

1 The Birth of Jesus the Messiah: Emmanuel

Matthew 1:18-25

LEARNING MENU
Keeping in mind the ways in which your class members learn best as well as their needs and interests, choose at least one learning segment from each of the three Dimensions.

Dimension 1: What Does the Bible Say?

(A) Read the text dramatically.

One of the challenges you may face as you lead the class in studying Matthew 1:18-25 is its familiarity. Because many class members are acquainted with the passage, they may assume that they already know all that it says. To open up the possibility of new learnings, ask four members of the class to present Matthew 1:18-25 as a dramatic reading.
- Read Matthew 1:18-25, either silently or aloud.
- Ask volunteers to take at least the two speaking roles in a dramatic reading of Matthew 1:18-25: the NARRATOR and the ANGEL OF THE LORD.
- If you and your class want to try acting out simple stage directions while dramatically reading the text, add two more volunteers for additional non-speaking roles: JOSEPH and MARY.

- If you try acting out the dramatic reading, either allow actors to add their own simple movements, or try the following.
—Begin with the NARRATOR standing in the background. MARY sits at left-center. JOSEPH stands at right-center. The ANGEL OF THE LORD is off-stage.
—As the NARRATOR reads verses 18-19, JOSEPH moves closer to MARY and stands over her, looking intently at her. Then he turns, walks away from her, sits down, and closes his eyes (to represent sleep).
—The ANGEL OF THE LORD comes to JOSEPH as the NARRATOR begins verse 20. The ANGEL OF THE LORD speaks his or her lines in verses 20-23, and exits.
—The NARRATOR continues to read verses 24-25 as JOSEPH opens his eyes and again approaches MARY, looking intently at her as he sits or kneels beside her.
- Invite class members to reflect on and discuss what they saw and heard. You might ask the following questions:
—What did you hear or see that was new?
—What did you hear or see that was confusing?
—What did you hear or see that was reassuring?
—What did you feel as you heard and saw the drama?
- If your class feels uncomfortable with reading this text dramatically, ask a volunteer to read Matthew 1:18-25 aloud while persons listen with their eyes closed and attempt to imagine the action taking place in the text. Then invite discussion based on the above questions.

THE BIRTH OF JESUS THE MESSIAH: EMMANUEL 3

(B) Answer the questions in the study book.

Class members will read each chapter and answer the questions in Dimension 1 of each chapter before the class session. However, some classes may wish to
—share and check their answers together during class
—discuss their answers as part of the class session
—work on answering the questions together during class

Spend the least amount of time necessary in looking at the questions and answers in Dimension 1. Dimensions 2 and 3 contain the "meat" of the chapter's material. Dimension 1 is intended only to get you started with reading and thinking about the biblical text.

Sometimes Dimension 1 questions will be open-ended, without any one definite "right" answer. At other times the questions should be easily answered by reading the text.

Answers to Dimension 1 questions in this chapter are
1. a righteous man (verse 19) and son of David (verse 20);
2. dismiss (divorce) her quietly (verse 19);
3. the message of the angel of the Lord (verses 20-23);
4. Isaiah 7:14.

Dimension 2: What Does the Bible Mean?

(C) Define key words.

Not everyone in your class will have a clear and common understanding of four key words used in this chapter: *genealogy*, *Messiah*, *Holy Spirit*, and *vocation*.
- Have at least one copy (but preferably four copies) of both an ordinary dictionary and a Bible dictionary.
- Divide the class into four groups.
- Assign a different key word to each group, asking the groups to prepare a brief definition of their term to share with the whole class.
- Share and discuss definitions.
- You may want to ask: Why might Matthew have considered it important to trace the genealogy of Jesus through King David to Abraham, as found in Matthew 1:1-17? Allow time for discussion of possible answers.

One answer may be that Matthew proclaimed Jesus as the Messiah because he fulfilled in his ministry what had been begun in Abraham and David.
—Abraham was the founder of the people of Israel; Jesus was the founder of the New Israel, the church.
—David was the embodiment of the ideal king in Israel's history; Jesus was the revelation of God's ruling presence in Israel and throughout the whole creation.
—Jesus is "son" of Abraham and "son" of David because Jesus fulfilled the work of creating and revealing the people of God.

Another part of the answer may be found in looking at the way the expression *son of* was used in the culture in which first century Israel was located. In addition to its obvious use to refer to a male child of a particular parent, this phrase also commonly indicated a person who embodied a certain characteristic or quality of life. For example, in first century Israel someone might have been called "son of rebellion," "son of righteousness," "son of strength." Today we might well say "child of" to be more inclusive.

Possibly, Matthew might have used the term *son of* in the genealogy of Jesus to emphasize the qualities found in Jesus' life as well as his biological lineage. In this case, Jesus is son of David and son of Abraham (Matthew 1:1) not just because of physical descent but also because his life revealed the faith of Abraham and the submission of King David to God's royal power
- If you want additional background information, read articles on "Abraham," "David," "genealogy," and "Messiah" in a Bible dictionary.

(D) Prepare a personal genealogy.

Consideration of Jesus' genealogy in Matthew 1:1-17 can be made more personal by looking at one's genealogy or family tree.
- Provide paper, pencils, or other writing materials.
- Allow time for class members individually to sketch on paper their own family trees as far back as they are able.
- Discuss:
—What makes you sons or daughters of a particular family?
—To what extent does physical descent make you a son or daughter of a particular family? To what extent does participation in a distinctive family quality of life make you a member of a particular family?
—What makes you a member of God's family?

(E) Consider God's miraculous interventions.

- Provide markers or chalk and a large writing surface or newsprint.
- Reread Matthew 1:18-25, either individually or with one person reading the passage to the whole class.
- Ask class members to note ways in this passage that God appears to intervene miraculously in the lives of people. List these ways on one side of the writing surface.
- Discuss: What makes an intervention of God *miraculous*?
- Ask class members to share ways in which they have experienced God's miraculous interventions in their own lives. List these ways on the other side of the writing surface.

(F) Look at Joseph as a role model.

- Provide markers or chalk and a large writing surface or newsprint.
- Ask class members to identify those traits found in Joseph that qualify him to be a role model for Christians.

(G) Explore the meaning of a revelation.

- Reread Matthew 1:18-25.
- Discuss: What is the role of the *angel* in this passage?
- If the point does not come out in discussion, tell the group that an angel of the Lord is a messenger from God. The appearance of the angel to Joseph in his dream stressed that what is said reveals God's will. Revelation is the self-disclosure of God. However, revelation requires response on the part of those who receive the revelation. Only "when Joseph awoke from sleep" did he do "as the angel of the Lord commanded him" (Matthew 1:24).
- Note that God's special revelation appeared again in dreams in
—Matthew 2:12, when the wise men are "warned in a dream not to return to Herod";
—Matthew 2:13, when an angel of the Lord appeared to Joseph warning him to take Jesus and Mary to Egypt to escape Herod; and
—Matthew 2:19-20, when upon Herod's death an angel of the Lord "suddenly" appeared again to Joseph, calling on him to return with Jesus and Mary to Israel.
- Ask class members to review their own lives for signs of turning points when something happened in which God revealed God's will in a way that seemed comparable to an angel of the Lord appearing in a dream. You might ask these questions:
—How does God's revelation occur in situations that require important choices?
—What are the guidelines that help you discern what God's revelation commands you to do?
—What are some social pressures preventing your ready response to God's revelation?
—What are some personal attitudes that promote your response to God's revelation?
—In what ways have you experienced God's revelation in your life when it produced conflict within yourself or with other people?

(H) Look at the significance of names.

- Provide one or more copies of books for naming a baby. These books are available at most book stores and give origins and meanings of common names.
- Invite class members to look up their own names or the names of their children in the name books. Ask them to share their name's meaning and brief stories about how they were named or how they named their children.
- Discuss to what extent names say something about the expectations held for a person.
- Reread Matthew 1:21 and 25.
- Note that the name *Jesus* is a variation of the name *Joshua* and means "he will save." In the original Hebrew and Aramaic, *Jesus* literally means *Savior*.
- Discuss: What do you think it meant for Matthew to recall Isaiah 7:14 with its association of naming a special child *Emmanuel* (see Matthew 1:23)?

(I) Share additional background on the Gospel of Matthew.

If your class is interested in additional information about this Gospel, you may want to share these items:
—The Gospel of Matthew was probably written sometime between the years 80 and 90 of the common era (C.E., also known as A.D. for the Latin words *anno Domini*, meaning "in the year of our Lord").
—The Gospel of Matthew was probably written in northern Syria, possibly in Antioch. (You might wish to have class members locate Antioch on a map.)
—This Gospel was written not merely to report on what happened during Jesus' earthly ministry. Rather it was written largely to help members of the Christian community in that region to be aware that the risen Lord continued to be present to them.
—Matthew's Gospel largely emphasizes that Jesus is our "Emmanuel," God present to us in the risen Christ, the ongoing revelation of God in our lives.

Dimension 3: What Does the Bible Mean to Us?

(J) Consider Emmanuel as our Judge.

- Read Matthew 2:1-23. Note especially verses 16-18.
- If your class is curious, you may note that Matthew 2:18 quotes from Jeremiah 31:15. Rachel was the wife of the patriarch Jacob. She died in childbirth. Genesis 35:16-20 indicates she was buried near Bethlehem.
- Discuss the following questions:
—What happened in Matthew 2:1-23?
—What thoughts and feelings do you have about this passage, especially verses 16-18?
—Are children today treated like those in this passage?
—Do you know of refugees fleeing from danger in ways similar to that of Joseph's family?
—Where do you think God is in such situations?
- Some Christians are uncomfortable with the notion of God as judge because they think that judgment is

incompatible with love. Ask class members to reflect on ways in which experiences of love bring to light those attitudes and actions in people's lives that are unloving.
- The more we experience Emmanuel—the revelation of God's love in Jesus—the more we are confronted with God's judgment of our failure to love. One of the signs of Christian faith is the willingness to admit that in our personal and communal lives, we often experience God's love as judgment.

(K) Consider Emmanuel as our Savior.

- Note Matthew 1:21 in which the angel told Joseph that Jesus "will save his people from their sins."
- Some persons misunderstand salvation. They only think of salvation as the experience of being saved *from* something. They do not think of exploring *why* they are being saved. However, we can say after reading Matthew's account of Jesus' birth that Jesus saved his people from their sins while revealing to them the presence of God in their lives.
- Ask class members to discuss the idea of being saved *for* something and not just being saved *from* something.

(L) Look at how salvation might be rejected.

- Discuss the notion that the experience of salvation involves a call to obedience.
- Divide the class into small groups of three or four. Ask the groups to dramatize a scene in which Joseph refused to do as the angel of the Lord commanded him. Consider a scene that would include a different dialogue between Joseph and the angel of the Lord, a scene that would convey an overwhelming desire on Joseph's part to follow the customs and rules of his society and religion, or a scene that would show the results of Joseph's refusal of Mary and her child.
- Ask the smaller groups to act out their dramatizations.
- Discuss these questions:
—In what ways would Joseph's refusal have been a tragedy even if the birth of the Messiah had not been at stake?
—What contemporary situations might lead to similar tragedies?
—What societal customs and religious rules prevent us from experiencing the fullness of salvation and God's presence among us?
—In what ways might we be saved from our sins as we are made aware of the will of God for our lives?
—To what extent is it possible to have faith in Jesus without doing the will of God for our lives?
—How often does the experience of God in our lives or our awareness of Jesus as the Messiah call us to service?

(M) Consider our responsibilities as we experience Jesus as Emmanuel.

- Provide markers and a large writing surface.
- Sum up the main point of this session—to explore how the birth of Jesus the Messiah fulfills God's promise to be with us, leading us to focus on how we experience God's presence in *our* lives.

The congregation for which Matthew wrote his Gospel was likely an affluent congregation. It may have been struggling with many of the issues confronting middle-class Christians today. Sometimes persons who enjoy economic security find difficulty in understanding and being sensitive to the needs of persons less well off economically and materially. Besides the proclamation of the birth of Jesus the Messiah, chapters 1 and 2 of Matthew's Gospel might also have challenged the members of Matthew's congregation to consider the needs of women and children who lived at risk within their society.

Like Matthew's congregation, if we are not sensitive and compassionate in the face of the needs of persons who are weak and powerless, then we will find difficulty experiencing God as our faithful companion.

- While you write their responses, ask class members to list those things they desire most in their lives.
- Then ask class members to estimate the percentage of their time and money they spend on the things they desire most in their lives.
- Move into a discussion of the extent to which concern for weak and powerless persons influences how we spend our time and money. Challenge class members to consider specific ways by which they can increase the percentage of time and money they spend on concern for weak and powerless persons.
- Discuss this question: In what ways does caring for the needs of persons who are weak and powerless improve our relationship with God and make us more open to the presence of God in our lives?

Additional Bible Helps

The role of women in the genealogy of Matthew 1:1-17 and the role of Mary in the birth narrative of Matthew 1:18-25 might show us a tradition of the early Christian community that is often overlooked.

Mary was not just a passive participant in the birth of Jesus the Messiah. Mary was an actor in her own right. The Bible text emphasizes the fact that her involvement was not dependent upon her relationship to her legal husband, Joseph, but rather was dependent upon the action of the Holy Spirit. The ordinary understanding of that time in which helpless women were dependent upon powerful men is reversed. Mary was the one in whom holy power was embodied. Joseph, on the other hand, participated in the divine action only to the extent that he received and obeyed the revelation that the child in Mary's womb was "from the Holy Spirit."

The fact that the promise of Emmanuel (Isaiah 7:14) was fulfilled in the conception and birth of Jesus without the cooperation of a human father strengthens this view. Nothing Joseph did led the church to the conclusion that "what had been spoken by the Lord through the prophet" (Matthew 1:22) had been fulfilled. In these passages Matthew preserved a tradition about the beginning of the church that gave women a position of prominence. Instead of the expected submission of women to men, God chose to use women as instruments of God's miraculous intervention in human history. In the sight of God women and men are equally in need of God's action in their lives. They are also equally capable of responding to that action so that God's promises are fulfilled in their lives.

Matthew's vision of the church as a liberating and inclusive community originated in the church's memory of the miraculous birth of Jesus the Messiah. This memory recalled God's intervention in the lives of women throughout Hebrew history in order to maintain the continuity of God's people from Abraham through King David to the birth of Jesus the Messiah.

The four women who appear in the genealogy in Matthew 1:1-17 reveal how God's intervention through them maintained the lineage of God's chosen people when the continuity of physical descent was broken. In this way Matthew affirmed that women and men are children of Abraham and heirs of King David not by virtue of biological descent but because of God's miraculous action in their lives. The chosen people are not simply those who are blood descendants of the patriarchs and biological children of the house of David, but rather those who have their origin in God. Thus when Matthew 1:21 declares that Jesus "will save his people from their sins," the words *his people* must be understood not in the exclusive sense of a particular national, racial, or religious group but in the inclusive sense of all God's children. The universal nature of the Great Commission of Matthew 28:18-20 is already found in the vocation of Jesus as stated in Matthew 1:21. And Jesus is qualified for this vocation because his birth is "from the Holy Spirit."

If you have time, you may want to help the class recall the decisive roles played by Tamar, Rahab, Ruth, and Bathsheba (the wife of Uriah). Keep in mind that Matthew's Gospel places high importance on the fulfillment of Old Testament Scripture. You might report—or ask persons or teams to report—on each of these women, telling how she was the agent of fulfilling God's promise.

- Tamar: Matthew 1:3; Genesis 38; Deuteronomy 25:5-6. The story of Tamar reports how a woman endangered in a male-dominated society took the initiative to correct a dangerous situation created by the neglect of a powerful male, Judah, her father-in-law. She acted alone, without male support, and broke through the boundaries that had been set for her by society. She is remembered and incorporated into the genealogy of Jesus as an instance of God's intervention in the history of Israel.
- Rahab: Matthew 1:5; Joshua 2; Joshua 6:22-25. Rahab was a prostitute who lived alone in her own house, outside the normal structures and boundaries of society. She protected two Israelite spies by giving them sanctuary in her home. In exchange for her kindness the spies promised to spare her and all her family gathered in her house when Jericho was sacked and destroyed. Thus a foreigner—a cultural and religious outsider—decisively acted in the history of the fulfillment of God's promises to Israel. Her actions, inconveniences without male assistance, are remembered in the genealogy of Jesus because they suggest the powerful action of God.
- Ruth: Matthew 1:5; the Book of Ruth. Ruth also was a foreigner. In a world where security for a female was acquired by relating to males, Ruth chose to leave her own family and her own country, binding herself to her Israelite mother-in-law. Ruth secured a place for herself among the people of God by her own wits. She is remembered in the genealogy of Jesus as an example of God's extraordinary action on behalf of Israel.
- Bathsheba, the wife of Uriah: Matthew 1:6b; 2 Samuel 11 and 12. The life of Bathsheba, wife of Uriah, was endangered because of the adulterous relationship initiated by King David. As the powerless partner in an affair instigated by a powerful male, she nevertheless was a threat to a male-dominated family structure. David "solved" the problem by arranging for the murder of Uriah and by making Bathsheba his legal wife. But she is not remembered as David's wife within the genealogy of Jesus, rather she is remembered as *Uriah's* wife. Thus the story affirms the role of a woman at risk within the preservation of the people of God.

When we read the stories of these four women in the light of the birth of Jesus the Messiah by Mary "from the Holy Spirit," we can glimpse that Matthew drew upon a tradition affirming women as agents of God's miraculous action. As we reflect upon their lives, we can see more clearly that God's intervention in our lives always awaits our faithful response and is never complete without our imaginative and creative obedience.

2
Matthew 3:13-17 4:1-11

The Baptism and Temptation of Jesus the Messiah: Son of God

LEARNING MENU

Keeping in mind the ways in which your class members learn best as well as their needs and interests, choose at least one learning segment from each of the three Dimensions.

Dimension 1: What Does the Bible Say?

(A) Answer the questions in the study book.

The answers to Dimension 1 questions for this session can be discovered by reading Matthew 3:13—4:11. These discussion starters may help your class' exploration of the questions.

1. Consider the difference between John's understanding of Jesus' vocation and Jesus' own understanding.

2. Look at how Jesus' baptism represented his choice to value what God wants rather than what people want. What is it like to struggle with what God wants us to do? What is it like to give priority to what is pleasing to God?

3. Look at how the words *Spirit* and *Son* occur both in the baptism and temptation stories. Note also that the "voice from heaven," the climax of the baptism stories, prepares the way for Jesus to hear and obey "every word that comes from the mouth of God." How does the conflict between Jesus and John prepare you for the conflict between Jesus and Satan?

4. Look at the conflict between truth and falsehood. The "voice from heaven" or "every word that comes from the mouth of God" represents for Jesus that which is true. The words that come from Satan confront Jesus with that which is false. The Scriptures, that which "is written," reveal to Jesus what is true and enable him to overcome what is false. Reflect on ways the Bible—what "is written"—helps class members choose between truth and falsehood.

(B) Look closely at Jesus' vocation.

Ask class members to draw pictures expressing their understanding of Jesus' vocation.
- Provide paper and markers or crayons for drawing.
- Compare pictures with the text of Matthew 3:13—4:11 to discover points of agreement and difference.

(C) Examine the ritual of baptism.

- Have on hand copies of your congregation's hymnal, worship book, or baptism ritual.
- Read Matthew 3:13-17 to set the context with Jesus' baptism.

- Individually, within smaller groups, or as a whole group if you are small in number, read through your congregation's baptism ritual—silently, in unison, or in parts.
- Identify parts of the ritual that help to clarify what is pleasing to God.

Dimension 2: What Does the Bible Mean?

(D) Consider John the Baptist as a model for Christian witness.

The first thing Matthew said about John the Baptist is that he "appeared in the wilderness of Judea, proclaiming 'Repent, for the kingdom of heaven has come near.'" The word *proclaiming*, since it is the first word describing John's activity, is the word Matthew stresses as most important for understanding John's ministry.

Matthew presented John as one whose primary function was to proclaim or preach. The picture that comes to mind is one of an official herald announcing the good news of a decisive event.

John's message is more important than his person. What John says sets him apart, not who he is.

- Provide copies of a Bible concordance for use by class members.
- Divide the class into groups of three to five persons.
- Ask small groups to read or review Matthew 3:1-17. Invite them to use a Bible concordance to discover and look up other Bible passages mentioning John the Baptist.
- Have small groups list as many characteristics of John the Baptist as they can substantiate using descriptions in the Bible.
- Next ask the small groups to summarize John the Baptist's basic message in one or two sentences.
- Small groups should then discuss the following questions:
—What characteristics or qualities of John make him helpful as a model for Christian witness?
—What about John helps you in considering how you might be a Christian witness?
- What other persons in your own experiences have brought the good news of God to you?

(E) Rewrite John's message in contemporary language.

John challenged his hearers with the message, "Repent, for the kingdom of heaven has come near" (Matthew 3:2). Sometimes Christians are so familiar with the wording of a Bible passage that they glide over it without fully understanding it.
- Divide the class into groups of three.

- Ask the small groups to put John's message found in Matthew 3:2 into contemporary language that has meaning for them.
- Share the results and discuss points at which the text becomes clearer and more precise for them by an updating of the language.
- If you have time, ask the same small groups to consider persons who are different from them because of social, economic, racial, or other differences. How might they share John's message in language that would communicate to those persons?

(F) Explore the meaning of *repent*.

The Greek word *metanoia* translated into English as "repent" means a change of mind. But the Hebrew word *shub* used by the prophets to call the people to turn from ungodly living to a life of obedience and trust in God means a fundamental, radical reorientation of one's life.
- Discuss the following:
—To what extent is it possible to change your mind without exhibiting any difference in action or behavior?
—To what extent is it possible to turn your body or an automobile without going in a new direction?
- Demonstrate the concept of repentance by asking class members to stand and all face one direction. Instruct them to turn around and face the opposite direction. To repent involves just that kind of turnaround in one's life. (Note: If not all class members are easily able to stand and turn around, then invite a physically able volunteer to demonstrate turning for the class.)
- Divide the class into three groups. Assign one of these texts to each group:
—Jeremiah 4:1-2; 26:3; 36:3
—Ezekiel 18:21-28
—Hosea 6:1-6
- Ask each group to report on how their passage provides an example of how the Hebrew prophets called people to repent.
- Share the following information in your own words:

In John's preaching, the word *repent* had a positive meaning. It suggested that human life has a new possibility because God's gracious rule has drawn near or is at hand. The presence of God empowers people to choose God's will for their lives and to do that which is pleasing to God. John's announcement that "the kingdom of heaven has come near" expressed this. The immediate presence of God's goodness enables people to bear fruit worthy of repentance—to do good works.

The expression, *the kingdom of heaven*, summarized the longing of the people for the fulfillment of God's promises in their lives. John's preaching affirmed that what had always been considered a future hope was now a present reality, because God acted decisively in Jesus the Messiah to provide for the total well-being of all God's children.

Since God had drawn near to the people in the birth of Jesus, John could invite the people to draw near to God by turning away from the deceit of sin.

(G) Consider how Jesus fulfilled all righteousness.

- Read Matthew 3:13-17.
- Note that Jesus stated that he sought baptism at John's hands "to fulfill all righteousness." *Righteousness* as used in the Bible does not refer to action conforming to absolute standards but to action meeting the requirements of a given relationship. Jesus' baptism fulfilled "all righteousness" because it appropriately expressed his relationship to God. He humbled himself in the presence of God and chose to serve God's people.
- Ask class members to identify persons in history and in their own experience who have exemplified the biblical understanding of righteousness as a right relationship to God and to God's creation.

(H) Enter into the wilderness.

- Read Matthew 3:1-3 and 4:1-2.
- Share the following information in your own words: Both John's ministry and Jesus' temptations involved the "wilderness." Matthew's first hearers would have recalled the wilderness wanderings of the Israelites. The wilderness symbolized any place where chaotic and destructive forces threatened. The symbol of the wilderness also reminded people that God's presence was always in those places that seemed the most dangerous.
  - Ask class members to talk in pairs to identify their own wildernesses. For us, wildernesses are not only desolate geographical locations but also feelings of despair and hopelessness.
  - Ask persons also to share in pairs how God became vitally real to them in some "wilderness."

(I) Memorize key Bible verses.

Some classes may wish to internalize portions of Scripture by memorizing them. Jesus kept in focus God's will for his life by recalling key Bible passages during his temptations. Key Bible passages may also serve to remind us of God's will for us.
- Ask persons to work in pairs to memorize one of the Old Testament verses Jesus recalled during his temptation in Matthew 4:4, 6, or 10.

Dimension 3:
What Does the Bible Mean to Us?

(J) Explore the nature of temptation.

- Read Matthew 4:1-11.
- Note that Jesus' hunger in the wilderness was a sign of his entering completely into our humanity.
- List on newsprint or chalkboard the "hungers" class members call out as motivating our actions.
- As a class or in smaller groups, discuss
—ways in which these hungers may be signs of God's gracious care for us.
—ways in which the denial of these hungers can lead to emotional or physical disorders.
—ways in which basic human hungers may lead us to seek immediate satisfaction in ways that separate us from God and from each other.
—ways in which inappropriate indulgence of hungers can lead to types of addiction.
- Discuss insights gained about the nature of temptation.

(K) Consider motivations for making choices.

- Read Matthew 4:1-4.
- Provide paper for class members to make their personal list of the desires of their lives. Ask them to write down honestly the hungers motivating their lives—what do they *really* want, not what they think they ought to want.
- As persons call out desires from their lists, write them down on newsprint or chalkboard.
- Ask the class to work on ranking the desires listed.
- Discuss the following:
—What are the standards for ranking these desires or hungers?
—To what extent do these standards have equal relevance or change their relevance as situations change?
—To what extent is it possible for us in the concrete decisions of our lives to discover what God wants for us and to choose what God wants as the highest good in our lives?
—How often might a person have to make a decision about choosing what God wants? Once and for all? Repeatedly?
—How does the example of Jesus' choices in the wilderness give us some guidelines for our own decision making within the wilderness experiences of our lives?

(L) Take a closer look at baptism.

- This learning segment may be especially helpful if you have also done learning segment (C), in which your class examined your congregation's ritual of baptism. It may also stand on its own.
- Ask class members to read or review the material in the section entitled, "God Is With Us in Our Baptism and Our Temptation," pages 16-17 in the study book.
- Note especially the statement: "I realized that the child's baptism was not a celebration of our acts or our words but a celebration of God's acts and God's words. What we did in the baptism was incomplete in the same way that John's preaching and baptism were incomplete."
- Divide the class into groups of three to five persons. Ask the small groups to discuss the following questions:
— Think about the most recent baptism you participated in or observed. To what extent do you think that baptism was "incomplete"?
— Did you consider yourself as a participant in or an observer of that baptism? Why?
— What does your congregation claim when it baptizes children? when it baptizes youth and adults who can speak for themselves?
— To what actions and provisions does your congregation commit itself when it makes its claims in a baptism?
— In what ways can you as individuals and your class as a group help a helpless child withstand the "voices of deceit in the world, live in dependence upon God, and fulfill all righteousness"? (See page 17 of the study book.)
— How is that which is begun in a baptism continued and fulfilled?
- Ask groups to share and discuss their findings within the whole class.

Additional Bible Helps

Recurring Themes in Matthew's Gospel
JOURNEY THROUGH THE BIBLE seeks to introduce persons to the content and meaning of the entire Bible. In order to help this process, encourage your class members to read and reflect on the Bible readings suggested in Dimension 4: A Daily Bible Journey Plan, found at the end of each chapter in the study book. Dimension 4 will help persons to experience the overall development within a particular book of the Bible, such as the Gospel of Matthew, and to discover how issues raised in one place in the book are often raised again in other parts.

For example, the baptism of Jesus that begins his public ministry prepares us to understand the emphasis on baptism occurring in the Great Commission at the end of the Gospel of Matthew (28:18-20). Use this example to alert class members to watch for connecting links in Matthew's story of Jesus. On the one hand, we are surprised to find that baptism centrally figures in the Great Commission. Baptism was not a part of Jesus' ministry nor involved in the disciples' instructions about their ministry until the Great Commission. On the other hand, the baptism of Jesus figured decisively as the inaugural event of Jesus' own public ministry. The command to baptize all nations "in the name of the Father and of the Son and of the Holy Spirit" at the close of Matthew's Gospel made explicit what was already implicit in Jesus' baptism at the beginning. The God revealed in the baptism of Jesus is the God who is with the church "to the end of the age."

The temptation conflict between Jesus and Satan provided another example as it foreshadowed the later conflict between Jesus and Peter in Matthew 16:21-23. In Matthew 4, Jesus is confronted with the temptation to use his relationship with God to protect himself from harm. In Matthew 16, when Jesus began to teach his disciples that he must suffer, be killed, and be raised, Peter rebuked Jesus, saying, "God forbid it, Lord! This must never happen to you." Poignantly, the new temptation comes from the mouth of a friend and follower. Yet the importance of the issue raised by Peter and the turmoil it caused in Jesus' heart and mind are revealed in Jesus' response to Peter: "Get behind me, Satan! You are a stumbling block to me; for you are setting your mind not on divine things but on human things." The conflict with Peter intensified and internalized the temptation already anticipated in the encounter with Satan in Matthew 4.

Jesus' temptation also helps the reader experience the struggle with Satan as a continuing reality in the lives of those who follow Jesus. The petition in the Lord's Prayer
   "Do not bring us to the time of trial,
      but rescue us from the evil one" (6:13)
takes on a deeper meaning when heard against the background of Jesus' own wilderness experience. The petition reminds those who pray not to underestimate the power of deceit to lead them into sin. They cannot overcome lies except by dependence upon the truth of God. Those who are complacent about their own power to withstand evil are doomed to fail.

Contrasting Jesus With Other Characters
Matthew developed his themes at points by vividly contrasting the attitude and actions of Jesus with the attitudes and actions of others. You may especially want to watch for this contrast developing between Jesus and Peter.

Peter was not just a specific individual in Matthew's Gospel; he also represented the whole church. On the one hand, Matthew portrayed Peter as someone who constantly failed to overcome evil. Peter was confident of his own ability to remain faithful. He claimed superiority over others who failed. Yet in Gethsemane he slept with the others while Jesus prayed. In the high priest's courtyard after Jesus' arrest, he frantically defended himself.

Finally, he denied Jesus, thinking he had saved his own life.

On the other hand, Jesus triumphed over evil. He was supremely confident in the power of God. He identified with those who failed and gave himself in service for them. In Gethsemane he prayed while his disciples slept. In the high priest's courtyard he calmly refused to defend himself. Finally, he denied himself, lost his life, and yet found his life.

The Role of Satan

In Hebrew usage the word *satan* referred to any kind of human or supernatural adversary. The word *satan* evolved into a proper name, which was translated into Greek as *diabolos*, which in turn has been rendered in English as "devil." Satan, or the Devil, in the New Testament refers to a being who tempts persons to evil and who opposes God and God's people.

Nevertheless, in both the Hebrew Bible and the New Testament, Satan, or the Devil, has only limited power in the face of the sovereignty of God. The New Testament expressed the belief in Jesus' victory over evil. As Matthew described Jesus' temptation and the recurring testing of Jesus and his disciples, Satan, or the Devil, was not a rival entity capable of withstanding the power of God.

Although Matthew took evil seriously, there was no supernatural power of evil by which human rebellion against God could be explained. Jesus' conflict with Peter in Matthew 16 implied that evil had no "real" existence except as humans chose to believe what was false and thus became the embodiment of Satan. When humans choose to live by the truth of God revealed in the Word of God, evil is banished from their lives and has no power over them. No one can avoid responsibility by saying, "the devil made me do it."

The Kingdom of Heaven

As you read through the Gospel of Matthew, you may notice that Matthew refers consistently to the "kingdom of heaven" instead of the "kingdom of God." In fact, Matthew uses the expression *kingdom of God* only five times: 6:33; 12:28; 19:24; 21:31; and 21:43.

Matthew may have preferred using the term *kingdom of heaven* because of the reluctance of devout Jews to use the name of God. Therefore he would have characteristically used the term *kingdom of heaven* in order not to offend Jewish-Christian members of the congregation or Jews whom he was seeking to attract to the congregation.

However, both expressions claim the whole of creation as the realm ruled by God. God's rule is not an abstraction but the reality of God's self-giving love present even now in Jesus the Messiah.

3

Matthew 4:12-25

The Ministry of Jesus the Messiah: Preaching

LEARNING MENU

Keeping in mind the ways in which your class members learn best as well as their needs and interests, choose at least one learning segment from each of the three Dimensions.

Dimension 1: What Does the Bible Say?

(A) Write a definition of *gospel*.

The word *gospel* or *good news* appears in Matthew 4:23. It is perhaps the most important word in the passage studied in this session.
- Divide the class into groups of three. Assign each group to write a one-sentence definition of either *gospel* or *good news*.
- As groups report their definitions, write them on newsprint or chalkboard.
- Consider the common and different features of the several definitions.
- If you have time, work as a whole group to arrive at a consensus definition of *gospel*.

(B) Answer the questions in the study book.

The answers to Dimension 1 questions for this chapter can be discovered by reading Matthew 4:12-25. These discussion starters may help your class explore the questions.

1. Speculate on why John the Baptist was arrested. To find out more about John's arrest and fate, you will want to read Matthew 14:1-12. Keep in mind that Roman Palestine in the first century did not operate under a constitutional legal system such as the United States and many other modern nations enjoy. Arrests, imprisonments, and executions may have had as much to do with power struggles as with law.

2. Look carefully at the prophecy cited by Matthew in 4:15-16. Note also how early generations of Christians might have understood Jesus to have fulfilled each phrase of this passage. You might also want to do some digging to see how the prophecy as found in Isaiah 9:1-2 was understood by its first hearers.

3. Note that the phrase *fish for people* is never actually explained in the Bible passage. Peter and Andrew, as well as the first readers of Matthew's Gospel, would have had to use their imagination to understand the phrase. What images does the phrase evoke for you?

4. Compare John's message in Matthew 3:1-12 with Jesus' message in Matthew 4:17-25. One significant point

13

is that the words *gospel* or *good news* do not appear in Matthew before 4:23. John the Baptist does not proclaim the Kingdom as "good news," but Jesus does. How does that fact affect your reading of the two messages?

Dimension 2: What Does the Bible Mean?

(C) Consider the implications of Jesus making his home in Capernaum.

Some of your class members may be surprised to read Matthew 4:13 and find that Jesus "made his home in Capernaum by the sea." The idea of Jesus actually having a home seems to contradict the statement of Jesus in Matthew 8:19-20 and Luke 9:58 that "Foxes have holes, and birds of the air have nests; but the Son of Man has nowhere to lay his head."

- After pointing out Matthew 4:13, discuss the following questions:
—What does it mean for your perception of Jesus that he evidently had a home just like most other persons in the ancient world?
—To what extent have you considered previously the possibility that Jesus might have kept a home?
- Be sure to help class members locate Capernaum on a map. A Bible dictionary or atlas can help your class members find additional information about Capernaum.
- Discuss the question: To what extent is it easier to deal with the demands of a Jesus who might have been a wandering migrant than with the demands of a Jesus who "made his home in Capernaum"?

(D) Explore the daily realities of Jesus as homeowner and homemaker.

- If you have not already done so, read Matthew 4:13, noting Matthew's claim that Jesus "made his home in Capernaum."
- Before this class session, browse through such resources as your church's Sunday school picture files and your church library for illustrations and articles about houses and home life in first century Galilee. Bring those resources to share in class.
- One possibility is to provide time for class members individually or in groups to use illustrations, books, and articles to prepare brief reports to share about houses and home life such as Jesus might have experienced.
- A quicker alternative is to summarize this information:
  "At every period covered in the Bible there was a variety of dwelling. The house of a free man or an official would face a street and adjoin other houses. It might be part of the city wall with a window opening to the outside (Joshua 2:15-21; 2 Corinthians 11:33). Probably it would be rectangular with an open court in front. The door would be of wood with a wooden beam as the lintel and two upright posts as jambs. There would be a room for domestic animals, sleeping quarters, and a central room with a hearth for cooking and braziers for heating. Smoke would go out through open windows, which could be closed by latticework. The ceiling would be of wooden beams plastered over with clay. Some of the flooring would be of plaster or stone. Steps would lead to the roof, where there would be a guest room (2 Kings 4:10). The surface of the roof would be of clay, which regularly had to be replenished and rolled, as in many houses today. In the spring grass might grow briefly on the housetop" (Psalm 129:6; Isaiah 37:27). (From "House," by O. R. Seller; *The Interpreter's Dictionary of the Bible*, Volume 2: E-J, Abingdon Press, 1962; page 657)
- Another helpful resource on this topic is *Jesus and His Times*, Reader's Digest Association, 1987; pages 230-232.
- Another alternative learning method is to ask class members to work individually, in teams, or as a whole class to construct a model of a first century Palestinian home from illustrations and research information. Provide cardboard, construction paper, scissors, and glue or tape. Be careful not to allow this activity to take up all the time you want to spend on this chapter.
- In any case, discuss the following questions:
—How might Jesus' home in Capernaum have represented a new way of defining "family" and provided new possibilities for the everyday activities that are carried out in a home?
—How might Jesus have made his home a place where the kingdom of heaven was realized on earth?

(E) Imagine how Jesus felt as he made his home in Capernaum.

- Use one or more of the following questions as discussion starters. Emphasize that students will need to use their imaginations to respond since we cannot know definite answers to these questions.
—What might have motivated Jesus to leave Nazareth?
—What kind of feelings might Jesus have had as he left his home and family in Nazareth?
—Why did Jesus choose Capernaum?
—How might Jesus have been received as he moved into his home in Capernaum?
—How might Jesus' home have seemed different from other homes in Capernaum?
—What kinds of activities might Jesus have pursued in his home?
- While we cannot know for sure about Jesus' home life either in Nazareth or Capernaum, he might possibly

have worked as a carpenter in his home. He probably preached and taught in his home. He might have opened his home to persons needing care and healing. His home might have become a gathering place for outcasts and others excluded from other homes. We can say with good certainty that Jesus, as a devout Jew, worshiped God in his home, offering thanks at meals and starting and ending each day with prayers he had learned as a child.

(F) Discuss what must be left behind to follow Jesus.

- Note that although Peter and Andrew left their homes and livelihoods in order to follow Jesus, not everyone necessarily has to do so. However, some things may need to be left behind.
- Listing responses on newsprint or chalkboard, ask class members to name things they believe must be left behind in order to follow Jesus.
- Possible responses may include destructive actions such as violence, self-indulgence, waste, careless speech, reckless behavior, and various forms of abuse. They may also name attitudes such as prejudice, complacency, indifference, self-righteousness, and bigotry.
- Discuss these questions:
—To what extent might persons be able to relocate their homes or change their jobs without changing actions and attitudes?
—To what extent might persons be able to stay in a particular location or occupation and yet change their actions and attitudes?

Dimension 3: What Does the Bible Mean to Us?

(G) Read the text personally.

The attempt to understand what the Bible means always involves considering what the Bible means *to us*. We bring to any biblical text our prior experiences, concerns, and preconceptions. There is no such thing as a neutral reading or hearing of a Bible passage. We read it or hear it always from our own point of view. All understandings of a Bible passage are subjective to some extent. Failing to acknowledge this factor often leads persons to claim that there is only one "right" way to read and hear the Bible and its message—usually their own way!
- Ask a class member to read Matthew 4:12-25 aloud.
- Permit a period of silent reflection, giving class members time to identify for themselves what is the most important part of the passage. Allow at least one or two minutes. Ask class members to jot down on a piece of paper the part they identified.
- Ask persons to share in turn the part they identified as most important in the Bible passage.
- If different parts are identified, discuss this question:
—Why have different persons identified different parts of the passage as the most important?
- If everyone agreed in their identification of a most important part of the Bible passage, then discuss these questions:
—Why do you think everyone in this class agreed about what part of this passage was the most important?
—To what extent do you think that persons differently situated from you in this class might select a different part of the passage as the most important?
- In either case, discuss these questions:
—What different interests and needs influence the way you understand the Bible?
—What do you think about the idea that there may be no one "right" way to understand a Bible passage?
—To what extent do you think an understanding of a Bible passage might be "wrong"?
—How might you be able to discern whether an understanding of a Bible passage was "wrong"?

(H) Reflect on where the gospel is in your home.

For most persons, homes are the places where basic decisions about their lives are made. These decisions involve economic activity, education, health care, and religion. Home can be settings where either good is affirmed and evil denied, or evil affirmed and good denied. Most persons have some control over the activities in their homes and can begin to act responsibly without waiting for some external authority to decide.
- Lead a discussion around one or both of these concerns:
—Even though many persons work outside their homes, homes are still the places where we usually make significant decisions about how to use the money we earn. Determining the household budget may be the most revealing activity in the home. How much we spend for various items in our budgets indicates with fair accuracy the priorities in our lives. Given the definition of *evangelical* as sharing or spreading the good news in ways consistent with Matthew 4:12-25, to what extent should we expect our household budgets to be evangelical? To what extent are our household budgets actually evangelical? To what extent have we examined the items in our household budgets in light of God's claim upon our resources? To what extent do our budgets and expenditures reflect our commitment to the kingdom of heaven?
—In what ways does the way you manage your household have to do with persons who are homeless? To what extent do we take our own homes for granted? In our commitment to the kingdom of heaven, how may we

become advocates and activists on behalf of persons who do not presently have homes?

(I) Imagine *light* as a figure of speech for Jesus and his disciples.

- While you list responses on newsprint or chalkboard, ask class members to talk about what *light* means to them.
- Next ask class members to identify some aspect of their own experience of Jesus that leads them to the conclusion that Jesus is the "light" for all people. In doing so, they may consider specific activities of Jesus and reflect on how those activities have become "light" for their own lives.
- Provide opportunity and supplies for persons to express the symbolism found by them in "light." You might provide supplies such as drawing materials and modeling clay.

Additional Bible Helps

Gospel or "Good News"
The Greek word found in Matthew 4:23 that is rendered in English as "gospel" or "good news" is *euanggelion*. From it we derive such words as *evangel, evangelical, evangelist,* and *evangelism. Evangel* is an English word meaning "the Christian gospel," although it is not commonly used today.

Jesus is the content of the *evangel,* of the gospel. One who follows Jesus is *evangelical* by definition. One who preaches and practices what Jesus preached and practiced is an *evangelist. Evangelism* is any activity serving or promoting the kingdom of heaven as revealed in Jesus. The standard for giving content to the words *evangel, evangelical, evangelist,* and *evangelism* is the enlarging and inclusive action of God on behalf of all God's creation.

Capernaum
Matthew 4:13 indicates that Jesus "left Nazareth and made his home in Capernaum by the sea." Not much is known about Capernaum with certainty except that it was located on the northwest shore of the Sea of Galilee. Probably, Capernaum was situated on a site now known as Tell Hum. Capernaum appears to have been named for a person named Nahum, though no evidence exists to link this Nahum with the Old Testament prophet.

In Jesus' time Capernaum was considered a city, much larger than Nazareth. The ruins at Tell Hum cover an area roughly a mile long. It was located near an east-west trade route.

Besides being the place where Jesus made his home and conducted much of his ministry, Capernaum was also the home of at least Peter and Andrew. Throughout the gospels Capernaum is named as the setting for several healings and other incidents.

Galilee
The word *Galilee* means "district." In Matthew 4:12-25, it appears as an abbreviated version for "district of the Gentiles" or "district of the nations."

At the time of the conquest of Canaan, the region was assigned to the Israelite tribes of Naphtali, Zebulun, and Issachar. After the Exile, the name *Galilee* included all of Canaan (Palestine) north of Samaria and west of the Jordan River. The Highway of the Sea passed through Galilee to Egypt and exposed the region to the rich cosmopolitan cultures of the first century world.

Galilee was called the "district of the Gentiles" because from earliest times, Israelites and later Jews lived there among non-Israelite and non-Jewish peoples. At the time of Jesus, Galilee was considered as a rather isolated region of Palestine, away from the political and cultural centers of Judea, and therefore particularly subject to the influence of Greek civilization. It was also a center for popular uprisings against Roman authority.

That major part of Jesus' ministry as portrayed in the Gospel of Matthew (also as portrayed in Mark, Luke, and John) occurred in Galilee. When Jesus moved from Nazareth to Capernaum to make his home there, he chose to settle among the Gentiles—a group mixed racially, politically, and religiously. Although Jews and Gentiles had lived together for centuries, at the time of Jesus the loss of political power and the spread of Greek culture made the Jews increasingly wary of all Gentiles. Jesus accepted the vocation of Israel to be instruments of God's salvation for the Gentiles and claimed it as his own vocation (read Isaiah 42:1-9; 25:6-8; 56:7; and Joel 3:12). However, opposition to the Gentiles persisted among some Jews who became followers of Jesus. The desire to combat this opposition is reflected throughout the Gospel of Matthew. When Matthew wrote his Gospel for the church in Antioch about 85 B.C.E., many members of the Christian community still considered Gentiles as morally and religiously inferior.

Since according to Matthew, Jesus is primarily concerned with preparing his disciples for the Gentile mission promised in the Hebrew Bible, his first task was to call the Jews to join him in that vocation. But he readily ministered among the Gentiles, received them into his home, ate and worshiped with them at the table. It is likely the case that from the beginning, Jesus' house in Capernaum was a home where Gentiles were welcomed and offered the hospitality of God's gracious presence. If this was indeed the case, then the Great Commission, given on a mountain in Galilee of the Gentiles in Matthew 28:16-20, called the disciples to become the "Jesus house" that they had already experienced when Jesus made his home in Capernaum. One way to conceive of the worldwide mission of the church is to think of it as the establishment of "Jesus houses" where all people receive the good news of the Kingdom.

Light as a Symbol or Image

Light is used in Isaiah 9:1-2 as a figurative expression for the inclusion of the Gentiles in God's promised salvation. One of the reasons for the choice of *light* as a metaphor for salvation is its universal application. All people who are sighted have an experience with light. Light is a symbol for life, freedom, well-being, fulfillment. Light is victorious over darkness, death, slavery, disease, deprivation. Matthew applied the Isaiah text to Jesus because he was convinced Jesus was God's promised salvation for all people—the "light" of the entire universe. He also chose light as a metaphor for salvation because he knew that all people, regardless of ethnic, cultural, or religious background, would understand the symbolic meaning of light.

Jesus is the "light" for "the people who sat in darkness" and "for those who sat in the region and shadow of death." The images of "darkness" and "the region of shadow of death" suggest the fate of prisoners locked up in dungeons and shut off from the source of life, the light. The text declares that Jesus' life and ministry are the "light" of God's presence and blessing because they bring liberation from all the powers of darkness that have held people in bondage.

Matthew came to these conclusions about Jesus because of the power revealed in Jesus' words and deeds. When Peter, Andrew, James, and John saw the "light" of God's presence and blessing in Jesus, they were liberated from the darkness of meaningless existence. They left everything and followed him. When "Jesus went throughout Galilee, teaching in their synagogues and proclaiming the good news of the kingdom and curing every disease and every sickness among the people," the "light" dawned "for those who sat in the region and shadow of death." The "light" led them out of the darkness of affliction, "and great crowds followed him from Galilee, the Decapolis, Jerusalem, Judea, and from beyond the Jordan."

The metaphor of light is taken up again in the Sermon on the Mount, in Matthew 5:14-16. But there it is applied to the followers of Jesus. What Matthew claimed for Jesus in 4:12-17, Jesus claimed for his followers as well. Using the same Greek word, *phos*, Jesus told his followers that their vocation was nothing less than his own vocation: "You are the light of the world." Just as they had experienced the grace of God's presence in him, so they had experienced in him God's call to service. Since they had received the blessing of the "light," they were qualified by the "light" to let their "light shine before others."

4 Matthew 6:1-21

The Ministry of Jesus the Messiah: Teaching

LEARNING MENU
Keeping in mind the ways in which your class members learn best, as well as their needs and interests, choose at least one learning segment from each of the three Dimensions.

Dimension 1: What Does the Bible Say?

(A) Answer the questions in the study book.

- The answers to Dimension 1 questions for this chapter can be discovered by reading Matthew 6:1-21. *Reward is the key concept to discuss in answering all four questions.* This text speaks plainly of the "reward" of righteousness. The word occurs seven times in Matthew 6:1-21.
- Matthew contrasts the reward of hypocrites—the praise given by others—with the reward of genuine righteousness given by God. The Greek word *misthos*, which is translated into English as "reward," means payment in return for a task of service rendered. "Treasures on earth" motivate hypocrites as the reward they seek and receive for giving alms, praying, and fasting. "Treasures in heaven" motivate the followers of Jesus to give alms, to pray, and to fast. These meanings of *reward* are radically different.
- Discuss: How do you see the difference between these two meanings of *reward* in your own life?

(B) Roleplay motives and rewards.

- Ask two class members to roleplay a scene in which one is a homeless person and the other is an affluent church member.
- Set the stage so that the homeless person sits on the floor with head bowed in distress. The affluent person walks by, stops, kneels beside the homeless person, speaks words of comfort and reassurances, and gives the homeless person money.
- Divide the class into groups of three persons. Assign one person in each group to be the affluent person. Assign the others the task of questioning the affluent person in order to discover what motivated the giving of money to the homeless.
- Ask groups to share motives as you list them on newsprint or chalkboard. Work together to classify each motive as "treasure on earth" or "treasure in heaven."
- Discuss:
—What are the external differences between an act performed for the praise of others and an act performed "in secret"?

18   JOURNEY THROUGH THE BIBLE

—How might one tell whether an act is performed to receive a reward from others or from God?

Dimension 2: What Does the Bible Mean?

(C) Diagram the Sermon on the Mount.

No part of the Sermon on the Mount can be studied adequately without considering the entire sermon, which extends from Matthew 5:1 through 7:27. Matthew recorded the sermon in such a way as to give the church at Antioch convenient access to the teaching of Jesus about the mission and message of the church.

- Divide the class into groups of three. Ask each group to devise its own diagram or outline of the Sermon on the Mount. The diagram or outline should cover the entire sermon, but it also should be in a form that will help persons recall the main points. The diagram or outline does not have to be in a straight line or outline form. Encourage creativity!
- One possible outline, reflecting the interweaving of key themes into the Sermon, might look like the following. Many other possibilities also are appropriate.

A1—5:3-10. Beatitudes. Who the disciples are.
  B1—5:11-16. The disciples' vocation.
    C1—5:17-19. Conditions for implementing the vocation.
      D1—5:20. Introduction of the disciples' righteousness.
        E1—5:21-47. The disciples' righteousness.
      D2—5:47-48. Conclusion of the disciples' righteousness.
      D3—6:1. Introduction of the disciples' righteousness.
        E2—6:2-18. The disciples' righteousness.
      D4—6:19-21. Conclusion of the disciples' righteousness.
    C2—6:22–7:11. Conditions for implementing the vocation.
  B2—7:13-20. The disciples' vocation.
A2—7:21-27. Who the disciples are.

Adapted from *The Gospel According to Matthew: A Structural Commentary on Matthew's Faith*, by Daniel Patte (Fortress, 1987; page 65).

(D) Demonstrate the meaning of "being with."

We often ask, "Are you with me?" when we are not sure how another person is understanding and identifying with what we are saying or doing. How might we respond if Jesus were to ask, "Are you with me?" in relation to his Sermon on the Mount?

- Ask for a member of the class to volunteer to play the role of Jesus as the authoritative teacher.
- Set the stage by asking class members to imagine that Jesus has just climbed up a mountain, sat down, and gathered them around him to teach them about the righteousness that "exceeds that of the scribes and Pharisees" (Matthew 5:20).
- Ask the person playing the role of Jesus to read aloud Matthew 5:38-42. Pause for a few moments of reflection. Then have the person in the role of Jesus ask the class, "Are you with me?"
- Point out that "being with" Jesus in this context means more than physical presence. It means "being with" Jesus both in the sense of understanding what he is saying to them and accepting Jesus' teaching as authoritative commandments that must be obeyed.
- Next, privately ask a volunteer to go up to the person in the Jesus role, publicly denounce Jesus as an "idealistic fool" in front of the class, and act as if he or she were striking Jesus on the right cheek. Instead of retaliating, have Jesus turn his other cheek also. Then have Jesus turn to the class and ask again, "Are you with me?"
- Discuss: To what extent are you willing to obey Jesus' teachings in the Sermon on the Mount as authoritative for your everyday life?

(E) Consider almsgiving.

- Summarize and share the following information: Many churches today have a practice of setting aside the coin offering each Sunday or a special offering on Communion Sundays as an emergency fund to relieve the subsistence needs of persons without other resources. While this is a commendable practice, it is not the same as almsgiving. First century Palestine had no state-supported system of welfare. The primary response of the community to the needs of widows, orphans, beggars, and persons with handicapping conditions was to give alms. On today's scale, almsgiving would be the equivalent of the entire range of public and private charitable institutions that our society has created to meet the needs of persons who cannot care completely for themselves.

    One of today's most important aspects of almsgiving is found in paying taxes to support the social programs set up by government to care for the needs of poor persons. This perspective suggests that as followers of Jesus we have a responsibility to know what these governmental welfare programs are, to support them willingly with our taxes, and to seek ways to make them more humane and more effective.

- Discuss the following:

—To what extent do you agree with this understanding of almsgiving?

—How might this understanding of paying taxes as almsgiving affect what you give to and through your congregation to help poor persons?

—What specifically might you do to help the poor to live with dignity as your brothers and sisters?

(F) Experience prayer.

Help your class experience prayer as communion with God, binding persons as members of God's family, rather than as an escape from human responsibilities. Your most important resource for leading your class into an experience of prayer is the Lord's Prayer.

- Summarize and share the following information: Careful study of the Lord's Prayer supports the conclusion that Jesus did not give it to his disciples as a form to be mechanically followed but as a model to be used creatively. The prayer itself is an example of *how* the disciples should pray rather than a prescription for *what* they should pray. Jesus did not introduce the prayer with the imperative, "Pray then in these words," but rather with the imperative, "Pray then in this way" (6:9).
- In small groups of two or three, discuss:
—What was Jesus alluding to when he introduced his prayer with the phrase, "in this way"?
—How well do most Christians pray "in this way"?
- All that Jesus teaches in this lesson about almsgiving, prayer, and fasting has a twofold objective:
  (1) To warn his disciples not to practice righteousness as an outward form and
  (2) To encourage them to practice righteousness as an inward disposition.

(G) Demonstrate the righteousness of hypocrites.

- Instruct the class to imagine itself in a worship setting. Ask one class member to volunteer to roleplay leading a worship service that is running overtime. Invite the class to assume the role of an anxious congregation. Some might look at their watches; others fumble with hymnals, Bibles, and bulletins. Still others might put on their coats. In the midst of the confusion, have the leader invite the congregation to pray the Lord's Prayer. The leader should rush through the prayer, accompanied by worshipers, who then quickly depart.
- Discuss:
—What thoughts or feelings does the "congregation" have? the "worship leader"?
—Did each feel righteous or hypocritical as they prayed?
- Remind class members:
—One can go through the motions of righteousness, even seem to follow the teaching of Jesus exactly, and still be hypocritical.
—The word *hypocrites* refers to those inside or outside the Christian community who practiced righteousness in order to pretend to be what they were not. The entire passage will be misused as a basis for making harsh judgments about others unless it enables the reader to see the hypocritical tendencies in his or her own life.

(H) Demonstrate the righteousness of the disciples.

A purpose of Jesus' teaching about righteousness may have been to help his followers see the connection between inward disposition and outward action. Everything depended upon the focus of the disciples. The authority of Jesus is sure because his life and teaching were such that his disciples wanted to follow him. They wanted the kingdom of heaven more than they wanted the praise of others. Their heart was fixed on treasures in heaven. Righteousness is authentic when it arises from a repentant and obedient heart, a heart transformed by God as revealed in Jesus. This truth is expressed in 7:15-20.

- Analyze the Lord's Prayer.
—Write (large enough for the class to see) the Lord's Prayer on chalkboard or newsprint. Phrase by phrase, discuss the intent of the prayer.
—The first phrase affirms God as "Our Father in heaven." The words mean that those who pray as Jesus taught begin by acknowledging that they are members of God's family and that God's unconditional goodness provides for their needs. The first three petitions ask God to help the disciples reaffirm and internalize their calling or vocation.
—"Hallowed be your name" sets as the goal of Jesus' followers the glorification of God, not only by the church, but by the whole world (5:13-16).
—"Your kingdom come" is a petition for the ultimate blessing, which the disciples receive when they practice God's presence by obeying the commandments of Jesus.
—"Your will be done, on earth as it is in heaven" asks God to grant that God's people will become obedient by appropriating Jesus' teaching as their supreme good.
—The last petitions ask God to provide the good things needed in order to do God's will on earth. "Give us this day our daily bread" means that the disciples can trust God to provide all that they need to be confident and single-minded servants of the Kingdom.
—"And forgive us our debts, as we also have forgiven our debtors" asks God to make disciples aware of their own evil and remove it so that they might be used by God to remove evil from others.
—"And do not bring us to the time of trial, but rescue us from the evil one" acknowledges the disciples' depen-

dence upon God in the struggle against evil and affirms God's goodness as the power that keeps them focused wholeheartedly on the will of God.
- With this analysis in mind, instruct each member of the class to compose a prayer in her or his own words, based on the teaching of Jesus about the way to pray. No words used in Jesus' prayer should be used in this exercise. Express Jesus' prayer in today's language.

Dimension 3: What Does the Bible Mean to Us?

The Sermon on the Mount is not an elective course for disciples. It is basic instruction for all who follow Jesus. The entire sermon, 5:1–7:29, is the "narrow gate" and the "hard road" that leads to life. Unless those who "talk the talk" of the Sermon on the Mount also "walk the walk" of the Sermon on the Mount they will "never enter the kingdom of heaven" (7:13-14; 5:20).

One of the meanings of this lesson for us is that we have allowed it to be removed from the center of our concern by other interests and other commitments. Perhaps the greatest challenge as you teach this lesson is the assumption of many that they have already obeyed Jesus' sermon. In order for the lesson to have meaning for us we must hear it as a call to repentance, which addresses us at the point of our need and offers us a new possibility. Exploring the text again can help us overcome our complacency of thinking the Sermon on the Mount makes no new and transforming demands on our lives.

(I) Hear the text and repent.

- Divide the class into three groups.
- Assign one passage to each group:
—Group 1, Matthew 6:1-4
—Group 2, Matthew 6:5-15
—Group 3, Matthew 6:16-21
- Each group should (1) read the text silently; (2) reflect on the text; (3) identify those things in the text that are heard for the first time or in a new way; and (4) identify the new behaviors that obeying the text requires.
- Each group should report findings to the larger class body. Findings may be recorded on chalkboard or newsprint so that the class will see the relationship between new learnings and new actions.

(J) Recognize and work for inclusive righteousness.

- Read and summarize the following information:
—The Sermon on the Mount was probably arranged in its present form in order to bring the traditions about the teaching of Jesus to focus clearly on a problem that had arisen in the church at Antioch. Antioch was a racially, culturally, religiously, and socially diverse urban center. All these different groups were represented in the Christian church and presented problems of prejudice and discrimination with which Christians had to cope in their daily lives. Christians, then as now, tended to reflect the distinctions that the larger community recognized. But the gospel called Christians to behave not according to the customs of the world but according to the will of God as revealed in Jesus.

—One of the major differences between the house of Jesus and the houses of the world was that Jesus included all in one family while the houses of the world excluded all who seemed to be different. The one thing that made the Christian community radically different from the world was that it was inclusive instead of exclusive. To be the "salt of the earth," Christians had to be inclusive (5:13). To be the "light of the world," they had to be inclusive (5:14). The inclusive action of God, who makes the "sun rise on the evil and the good, and sends rain on the righteous and the unrighteous" (5:45) set the example.

—Those who would exclude others are identified in the Sermon on the Mount as "scribes and Pharisees." Who were they? If we identify them as some group outside the Christian community, then we are almost certain to use this Scripture to make harsh judgments about others. "Scribes and Pharisees" must not be identified with a specific group of Jewish leaders. They represent any group of people, either inside or outside the church, whose attitudes and actions exclude others from their lives. The "scribes and Pharisees" function in the same way as the "hypocrites." They are a mirror in which our own exclusive attitudes and actions are reflected. They are not intended to be a magnifying glass for analyzing the failures of others.

- Discuss the difference between the disciples' righteousness and that of the scribes and Pharisees.
—What did it mean to the first disciples to "exceed" the righteousness of the "scribes and Pharisees"?
— What does it mean to today's disciples? (One interpretation is that it means to include those previously excluded or left out.)
- Read 5:21-28.
- Discuss:
—What one thing do the examples of inclusive righteousness, mentioned in the passage, have in common?
—Each example emphasizes the responsibility of disciples to restore relationships with people who would ordinarily be excluded from their concern. The passage reminds us to seek reconciliation, not vindication. Strive for pure thoughts, not justification. Accept responsibility for others, not privilege. Speak with integrity, not with pompousness. Offer generosity, not retaliation. Love unconditionally, not conditionally. The use of

Scripture, "You have heard that it was said to those of ancient times," to condemn others and to protect oneself from them is contrasted with Jesus' authoritative teaching that affirms the needs of others and responds to those needs in acts of love.
- Return to the same small groups used in (I), page 21. Identify the assumptions of the Sermon.

—Disciples of Jesus will want to obey Jesus.
—Disciples will be able to do what Jesus commands.
—Disciples want to obey Jesus because they want to enter the kingdom of heaven more than they want anything else.
—Disciples are able to obey Jesus because Jesus is with them, revealing God's presence in their lives. Since God is all inclusive, they are brothers and sisters of one family.

Additional Bible Helps

The Gospel of Matthew never mentions the teaching ministry of Jesus' disciples until the Great Commission: "All authority in heaven and on earth has been given to me. Go therefore and make disciples of all nations, baptizing them in the name of the Father and of the Son and of the Holy Spirit, and teaching them to obey everything that I have commanded you. And remember, I am with you always, to the end of the age" (28:18-20).

Matthew's assumptions are clear:

(1) Jesus is the authoritative teacher of the church. Jesus understood his role not only as a final judge at the end of history but also as the one empowered by God to "save his people from their sins"(1:21).

(2) Jesus' teaching ministry equips the church for its mission or vocation.

(3) Jesus' teaching is the content for the teaching ministry of the church.

(4) The teaching of Jesus is to be obeyed by all the nations, not just by the leaders of the church.

(5) The church is empowered for ministry by remembering that Jesus, the authoritative teacher, is always present.

(6) The church interprets Jesus' teaching correctly when it reads Scripture in light of an absolute commitment to the welfare of others.

(7) The church misinterprets Jesus' teaching when it reads Scripture to claim special privileges for itself, or particular racial, social, national, or religious groups.

(8) Scripture is correctly used by the followers of Jesus when it makes them want to love and helps them to do what love requires.

5 The Ministry of Jesus the Messiah: Healing

Matthew 8:1-17

LEARNING MENU

Keeping in mind the ways in which your class members learn best, as well as their needs and interests, choose at least one learning segment from each of the three Dimensions.

Dimension 1: What Does the Bible Say?

(A) Answer the questions in the study book.

The answers to Dimension 1 questions for this chapter can be discovered by reading Matthew 8:1-17. *The key concept is that Jesus fulfilled the legislation concerning clean and unclean mentioned in Leviticus 13–14.* He fulfilled the law by reinterpreting it in light of God's inclusive love.

Matthew reports that Jesus gave up privilege and status to be the agent of God's mercy. "He took our infirmities and bore our diseases" (17). God's laws were fulfilled not by using them to exclude or condemn others but by applying them as God's call to commitment to doing God's will, "on earth as in heaven."

- How did Matthew come to this radically new understanding of Scripture? The answer is contained in these texts, which preserve the traditions about what Jesus said and did.
- Focus your lesson plan on helping class members reflect upon what Jesus said and did when he "cured all who were sick" (16).

(B) Dramatize the Bible passage.

- Choose members of the class to portray the parts of the NARRATOR, the CROWDS, the LEPER, and JESUS as found in 8:1-4.
- Before the scene is enacted, instruct the class to listen and watch for what is new, confusing, or disturbing.
- After the dramatic portrayal, record the reactions of the class on chalkboard or newsprint.
- Again, choose class members to roleplay the parts of the NARRATOR, CENTURION, JESUS, and THE DISCIPLES as found in 8:5-13. Follow the instructions used in dramatizing 8:1-4 (above.)
- Select actors from within the class to represent JESUS, PETER'S MOTHER-IN-LAW, THOSE WHO BROUGHT DEMON-POSSESSED PERSONS, and THE SICK. Set the stage to contrast the order in Peter's house with the confusion created by those gathered outside. Since there is no dialogue in this section, a NARRATOR will read the text as found in 8:14-17, as actors silently portray the scene.

- After the dramatic portrayal, record again the reactions of the class on a chalkboard or newsprint as they reflect on what in the passage was new, confusing, or disturbing.

Dimension 2: What Does the Bible Mean?

(C) Consider healing.

- Summarize for the class the following information:
—Some argue that Jesus' ministry resulted in his becoming unclean in those instances where he touched the unclean. Matthew indicates, however, that whether he healed by touch or by word, "he took our infirmities and bore our diseases." By associating with those considered unclean or impure, Jesus took upon himself the stigma of their condition. In ancient times emotional and physical diseases were thought to be the result of evil powers that rendered the afflicted person unclean.
—These texts seem to proclaim that the power of evil to render people unclean or impure was broken by the power of good to cleanse and purify people and include them in the family of God. Since all that Matthew had reported reflected the faith of the church in the power of the crucified and risen Lord, it is not an exaggeration to say that the power to heal is the power of the cross. The same power is manifest whether the cure is accomplished by Jesus' word or touch. In his presence, evil was rendered powerless; cleanliness was the victor over uncleanliness. Uncleanliness no longer separated people from God or each other. The self-giving love of Jesus cleansed and purified all and equipped all for the service of God.

(D) Locate Antioch on the map.

- Using the map in the *Bible Teacher Kit*, page 149, available through Cokesbury, or using another good map of first century Palestine, locate the city of Antioch.

(E) Describe Antioch of the first century.

- Summarize the following information for the class:
—At the end of the first century C.E., Antioch's population totaled 150,000. The city was about two miles long and one mile wide, enclosed as a fortress by walls. The population was about 205 persons per acre.
—In this overcrowded condition, most people lived in tiny cubicles on narrow streets. Water was in short supply and was carried in jugs from public reservoirs. It was untreated, stagnant, polluted, and often undrinkable. There were no sewers. Chamber pots and pit latrines served the population.
—Houses were largely smoky, dark, dirty, and damp. The stench of feces, sweat, urine, and decay was everywhere.
—Streets were littered with garbage and manure. Human corpses (adult and infant) were abandoned in the street.
—Antioch was a breeding ground for infectious disease. Deadly epidemics raged for years, killing 20-30 percent of the population each time. The majority of the population suffered from chronic health problems that cause pain, disability, and ultimately death. Symptoms of disease, such as swollen eyes, lost limbs, and skin rashes were commonplace.

(F) Imagine yourself as a first century citizen of Antioch.

- In small groups of three to five, discuss the following situation:
—If we were citizens of first century Antioch, the things we would interpret as "good news" would be . . . . (List your findings on newsprint and share with your entire class).
- When small groups have reported on their discussion within the larger class setting, the leader should summarize the following information:
—The healing ministry of Jesus was good news to people who experienced sickness and death each day. The notion that God was with people in misery as a compassionate and caring presence was new in the pagan world. Equally revolutionary was the Christian insistence that because God loved people in their need, Christians could not please God without loving and serving one another.
—The practical expression of this proclamation in Antioch was that Christians behaved differently from pagans when epidemics, famines, natural disasters, and social upheavals threatened the city.
—Dionysius, bishop of Alexandria, in his Easter letter of 260 C.E. wrote: "Heedless of danger, they took charge of the sick, attending to their every need and ministering to them in Christ, and with them departed this life serenely happy . . . . Many, in nursing and curing others, transferred their death to themselves and died in their stead . . . . The best of our brothers lost their lives in this manner.

"The heathen behaved in the very opposite way. At the first onset of the disease, they pushed the sufferers away and fled their dearest, throwing them into the roads before they were dead, and treated the unburied corpses as dirt." (From "Antioch as the Social Situation for Matthew's Gospel," by Rodney Stark, *Social History of the Matthean Community: Cross-Disciplinary Approaches*, ed. by David L. Balch, Augsburg Fortress, 1991; pages 202-203.)

—The elementary nursing of the sick by Christians greatly reduced the death rate during epidemics.

—The Christian alternative to flight from disease may be the great miracle of urban life in the first century. The Christian community, motivated by the good news of the Kingdom, combined prayers and soup in a ministry that extended the word and touch of Jesus. Unclean people who were dying in stinking hovels were included in the Jesus house and nursed back to life. What Jesus had done long ago in Galilee, his followers continued in Antioch. They took the infirmities of others and bore their diseases.

(G) Discuss the necessity of praying and caring for the sick.

- Divide the class into small groups of three to five to prepare a prayer for those who are victims of the AIDS epidemic. Encourage class members to pray for all of the victims of AIDS. Include mention of persons of different sexual lifestyles, drug addicts, those infected by contaminated blood, and children.
- Discuss the power of prayer to commit Christians to action.
—Is prayer, without a decision to reach out to those considered "unclean," a force for good or evil?
—Can one pray effectively without offering one's self as an agent for fulfilling the petition?

(H) Discuss healing as enlargement of community.

- Summarize the following information for the class:
—The Christians of Antioch provided a healing ministry to brothers and sisters, to persons of every class and condition, including their enemies. They used their wealth and power to help those in need without consideration of class, race, religion, sex, or race.
—Mercy, considered by classical philosophers as a pathological emotion and character flaw was required of all Christians as the highest virtue. The Apostolic Constitutions, an anonymous early church document, outlines the responsibilities of deacons as follows: "They are to be doers of good works, exercising a general supervision day and night, neither scorning the poor nor respecting the person of the rich; they must ascertain who are in distress and not exclude them from a share in church funds, compelling also the well-to-do to put money aside for good works."(From "Antioch as the Social Situation for Matthew's Gospel"; page 200.)
—The revitalization of the ancient world did not come from a reform of paganism but from the revolutionary community of the disciples of Jesus. They offered healing and renewal in Antioch because their life together was stripped of all discrimination by the customs of the Jesus house. No one has said it more clearly than Rodney Stark: "To cities filled with the homeless and the impoverished, Christianity offered charity as well as hope. To cities filled with newcomers and strangers, Christianity offered an immediate basis for attachments. To cities filled with orphans and widows, Christianity provided a new and expanded sense of family. To cities torn by violent ethnic strife, Christianity offered a new basis for social solidarity. And to cities faced with epidemics, fires, and earthquakes, Christianity offered effective nursing services . . . . Once Christianity did appear, its superior capacity for meeting these chronic problems soon became evident and played a major role in its ultimate triumph" (page 205).

(I) Discuss the power of healing today.

- Roleplay a scene in the emergency room of a hospital. Choose class members to roleplay the part of a doctor, nurse, and patient. The patient limps into the emergency room with a severely infected knee. The nurse examines him or her and gathers information about the accident that caused the injury and led to infection. The nurse also questions the patient about his or her financial situation. The patient is unemployed and without health insurance or other financial resources. The doctor is called in. After examining the knee, the doctor prescribes an expensive antibiotic to combat the infection. The patient asks the doctor how much the antibiotic will cost. The doctor replies, "About fifty dollars." The patient departs, mumbling that there is no way to buy the prescribed medicine.
- Following the roleplay, lead the class in reflecting on this situation.
—Is universal health care a cause that should be supported by the Christian community?
—What can Christians do as we wait for reform of the health care system as we know it?
—How do the stories about the healing ministry of Jesus help us to respond to situations such as this?
—What opportunities avail themselves to Christians when they become involved with problems such as inadequate health care? What roadblocks are presented?

(J) Discuss healing as a qualification for ministry.

- Summarize the following:
The good news of the Kingdom gave those who heard and obeyed its message a life of meaning and purpose. The epidemics that brought chaos, fear, and despair to the pagan world were received by Christians as opportunities.

- Explore ministry to AIDS patients as a form of modern discipleship. Roleplay a crisis within a congregation created by the fact that the son of a faithful family has just tested HIV positive. From within your class, choose individuals to portray a pastor, father, mother, and son. This family has come to the pastor to seek support in dealing with this tragedy. Involve the class in suggesting how the pastor should respond.
— What are the needs of the parents? the son?
— How will the congregation prepare to meet this crisis?
— Does the healing ministry of Jesus shed light on this crisis and point the way to doing what is appropriate?
— Does an appropriate response always involve leaving everything to follow Jesus?

Dimension 3: What Does the Bible Mean to Us?

(K) Discuss healing as restoration to community.

A recurring theme in this lesson is that the healing ministry of Jesus involved restoring to the community those who were afflicted. Persons were never cured by Jesus in isolation from others; the cure was accomplished by restoring broken relationships and overcoming alienation. The sick and demon possessed were not first cleansed and then incorporated into the community. Rather they were included in the community by the compassion of Jesus and then declared clean. It is possible to conclude that people were made sick or infirm by the breaking of relationships that were necessary for their well-being, health, and salvation. When relationships were restored, these persons were made whole.

What might be a modern comparison? It is generally accepted that a large number of persons suffering from mental illnesses should not be confined in institutions but helped to lead useful lives in their own communities. Tragically, this insight has resulted in sometimes removing the mentally ill from institutions and placing them in some communities, which, because of ignorance or prejudice, would not or could not provide them the resources for living independent and fulfilling lives. Instead of providing a richer life, the plight of some mentally ill persons has worsened. Individual case workers among the mentally or emotionally ill provide some of the services required by those ill to function in society. Despite their dedication, however, mental health professionals cannot fully meet the need of these ill persons. What is required is that society at large become aware of the ill as brothers and sisters and include them in acts of compassion.
- Identify:
— What resources that might benefit the mentally or emotionally ill of your area are readily available in your congregation?
— What resources might you cultivate for the purpose of aiding the ill?

(L) Discuss healing as enlargement of community.

- Identify class members' viewpoints regarding the criminal justice system. Allow in your lesson sufficient time for members to share how reforms might best be made, using the information provided below as you find it helpful. Keep in mind that crime touches all of us to some degree. Some in your class may have particularly strong opinions about the criminal justice system (based perhaps on personal experience). Do not work for consensus or agreement in your discussion. Instead, strive to identify how Jesus' ministry enlarged community.
— Crime is a social disease that threatens the health of our communities. Few believe prisons to be primarily environments of healing or rehabilitation. The exclusion of criminals from community life has not reduced crime nor made communities safer.
— One of the recent developments in criminal justice has been the insistence of many judges that sentences be reviewed or reformed. Some judges believe that persons guilty of violence be incarcerated without possibility of parole. Some believe that nonviolent criminals be supported and kept within their own communities in hopes that they will become productive members of society. Alternative sentences for nonviolent offenders is not only a more effective means of rehabilitation than imprisonment, it is also less costly.
- The healing ministry of Jesus may provide Christians with the motivation and commitment to support humane and creative treatment of criminals.

(M) Discuss healing as qualification for ministry.

- Summarize the following story:
    A group of Christians in Indiana organized a march protesting the death penalty. Each person involved in the march was a member of families who had lost relatives through murder. While one might suspect that families of murder victims would favor the death penalty for violent crime, these did not. They had been delivered from hatred, desire for vengeance, or trust in violent solutions.
- Ask your class:
— Is there greater integrity when persons who choose to be participants in dealing with a social problem have themselves been hurt by the problem? Why or why not? Persons who participate in the healing ministry of Jesus

by becoming agents of his healing touch are qualified by the fact that they have been healed by Jesus' touch. The result is that they follow him "on the way" of the cross.

Jesus was able to heal because he renounced all earthly power, trusted the power of God, and fulfilled his vocation by making God's will his will. Disciples are able to heal because they leave everything, follow Jesus as Lord, and obey his word. We cannot become agents of the healing ministry of Jesus on our own strength, on our own terms, on our own wisdom. One of the practical consequences of being healed by Jesus is that we are delivered from the desire to use violence to punish those who have harmed us.

Additional Bible Helps

Some class members may be fascinated by the frequent reference to demons and the fact that Jesus *exorcised*, or cast out, demons. The text understands the existence of demons or evil spirits as beings that influenced human beings negatively.

The New Testament distinguishes between sickness and demon possession; however, at times it comes close to equating one with the other (Matthew 9:32-34; 17:15-18).

The healing ministry of Jesus included deliverance from physical and psychological disorders and from demon possessions. In some instances, physical illness was attributed to demon possession.

What did Matthew intend his readers to understand when he reported that Jesus cast out demons?

—The stories proclaimed that the power of the kingdom of heaven delivered people from the power of evil.

—The power of the kingdom of heaven was so superior to the power of evil that evil could not resist it.

—Jesus had the power to cast out evil not because of magic but because of his faith in God.

—Ultimately, the narratives were intended by Matthew to proclaim the good news of the Kingdom and to strengthen the faith of the church. The church benefited through the reminder that God's power was on the side of good, not evil. Evil was powerless in the presence of good; the power of good was absolutely trustworthy.

—Jesus did not hold those who were possessed by demons responsible for their condition. Instead of judging them harshly, he responded to the possessed as he did to all others who were diseased. He cast out the demons and cured the sick as expressions of his healing ministry.

—Faith in the Kingdom was the consequence of Jesus' healing ministry. Jesus was not able to heal people because of their faith; people were able to have faith because Jesus healed them.

—The texts remind us that people struggle with evil for which they are not responsible and with which they are unable to cope. Instead of judging others harshly or excluding them from Christian compassion, we are called by Jesus to respond to their need and to offer them the power of good that can deliver them from evil.

—These texts do not explain evil. They put us in touch with the power of God in the self-giving love of Jesus that delivers us from evil and equips us to be agents of that power. God does not compromise with evil.

—These texts rally around the power of good and assure us that evil is absolutely powerless to withstand the onslaught of good in the gospel of the Kingdom. The only question these narratives should raise is, "Do we believe in the gospel?"

—Honesty requires us to admit that often our actions reveal that we have trusted the power of violence more than we have trusted the healing touch of Jesus' love.

—Instead of speculation about demons, let us hear these narratives as a call to repentance, a call to turn from despair, a call to hope grounded in the victory of God's love over all that threatens human life.

—Repentance is costly because it requires us to give up our false security, to leave everything in order to claim the blessings of the kingdom of heaven.

—Reward is great because, as we seek first the Kingdom we discover that God provides everything that we need (6:25-34).

• Close your session with prayer.

6. The Ministry of Jesus the Messiah Accepted: Authority to Preach and Heal

Matthew 9:35–10:25

LEARNING MENU

Keeping in mind the ways in which your class members learn best as well as their needs and interests, choose at least one learning segment from each of the three Dimensions.

Dimension 1: What Does the Bible Say?

One of the most vivid pictures in this lesson is created by the imagery of Matthew 9:36. "When he saw the crowds, he had compassion for them, because they were harassed and helpless, like sheep without a shepherd." Jesus believed that Scripture was fulfilled not by judging or excluding the "harassed and helpless" but by loving them and including them (9:35-38). Only then would they recognize their shepherd and receive the blessings of heaven.

(A) Read the text dramatically.

- Read Matthew 9:35–10:25 silently.
- Ask two volunteers to take the two speaking roles (the NARRATOR and JESUS) and read the passage dramatically.
- If you or your class want to try acting out the passage using simple stage directions while dramatically reading the text, add more volunteers for additional nonspeaking roles: the DISCIPLES and the CROWDS.
- Invite class members to reflect on and discuss what they saw and heard. Ask the following questions:
—What did you hear or see that was new?
—What did you hear or see that was confusing?
—What did you hear or see that was reassuring?
—What did you feel as you heard and saw the drama?

(B) Answer the questions in the study book.

Preferably, class members will read each chapter and answer the questions in Dimension 1 before the class session. However, some classes may wish to
—share and check answers together during class
—discuss their answers as part of the session
—work on answering the questions together during class.

Spend the least amount of time necessary in looking at the questions and answers in Dimension 1. Dimensions 2 and 3 contain the "meat" of the chapter material. Dimension 1 is intended only to get you started with reading and thinking about the biblical text.

Dimension 1 questions may be open-ended, without one "right" answer. At other times the questions may be answered easily by reading the text. Answers to Dimension 1 questions in this chapter are

1. The crowds had no one to lead or protect them.
2. The "harvest fields" referred to the crowds. The "Lord of the harvest" was Jesus himself. Jesus saw in the crowds many who would respond to the gospel. The task was so urgent the harvest could be lost without sufficient reapers.
3. Matthew referred to a house as "worthy." Today we might equate "worthy" with "welcome." If the disciples were welcomed (extended hospitality), they were to stay and share the message of the gospel. If they were not welcomed, the house was not "worthy" in spirit—in which case, the disciples were encouraged to move on.
4. A follower could not anticipate better treatment than was granted to the teacher.

Dimension 2: What Does the Bible Mean?

(C) Create visual reminders.

- Provide modeling clay, paper, and crayons.
- Remind the class that the theme holding this lesson together is the sending forth of the disciples into the world for the purpose of ministering to the masses. The Twelve were equipped to participate in Jesus' ministry and were sent out with detailed instructions about where, what, and how they were to minister.
- Invite the class to use the art materials to create an expression of people who are "harassed and helpless."
- Invite class members to display their art projects, perhaps sharing basic information about them with a partner. You may want to create a worship center in the classroom, featuring the art pieces.

(D) Define key words.

Lead the class in a discussion of the relationship between the "good news of the kingdom" and all the needs of the people. Note that everything Jesus did in this text was motivated by his compassion for the crowds, "because they were harassed and helpless, like sheep without a shepherd" (9:36). The church is represented in these verses by the "twelve" and was created by the compassion of Jesus to be the instrument of that compassion.

- Study the meaning of the word *compassion*.
—The Greek translation for "had compassion" literally means "moved by one's bowels"; it was regarded by the Greeks as the seat of the more violent passions, such as anger and love.
—The Hebrews understood the bowels to be the seat of tender affections, especially kindness, benevolence, and pity.
—In this context, "had compassion" may mean that Jesus was moved in his innermost being by the plight of the "harassed and helpless" sheep.
—Jesus' compassion was overpowering, expressed in self-giving action. The word *compassion* is used four times in Matthew to describe the feeling that motivated Jesus' actions (9:36; 14:14; 15:32; 20:34). The word *pity* is used in 18:27, the parable of the unforgiving servant, to portray the emotion that moved the king to forgive his servant.
- Discuss the ways that we experience compassion today.

(E) Share personal stories of compassion.

- Divide the class into groups of three.
- Invite members of each group to share personal experiences of receiving compassion.
- Reassemble as a class and discuss the following questions:
—Is it possible to receive compassion if it is not expressed by appropriate action?
—What kind of feelings are generated by experiencing compassion?
—Do our memories of having received compassion motivate us to act with compassion?
—Is it possible to extend compassion if you have not experienced compassion?

(F) Share additional background information.

Share the following information.
—Matthew may have used the traditions surrounding the historic Jesus and his disciples, which originated shortly after the death and resurrection of Jesus, to address the problems in the church of Antioch about 85 C.E. These texts, therefore, suggest that Matthew understood the Christian community as a movement that arose out of the life of Jesus and that was designed to continue his mission. *These texts are dynamic rather than static because they help the reader to experience Jesus not merely as a memory of the past but as a living presence whose word continues to direct the people of God.*
—The church in Antioch was in danger of becoming "harassed and helpless, like sheep without a shepherd."
—The "shepherd" in this context referred to God, the owner and protector of the people. Israel had forgotten that it belonged to God, was defended by God, and was directed by God. The people were confused, powerless, and purposeless. Jesus could keep the church from repeating the history of Israel. He did this not by ignoring or condemning Israel but by calling his disciples to share in extending ministries of compassion "to the lost sheep of the house of Israel."

—Matthew was convinced that the church was constituted as the reformed people of God through two acts of Jesus. It was summoned (10:1) and sent out (10:5). The first act gathered and equipped the church for ministry; the second act gave the church its marching orders.

—By using the number *twelve*, to refer to the inner core of Jesus' disciples, Matthew reminded the church that it was the fulfillment of God's promise to bless the Gentiles through the twelve tribes of Israel.

(G) Affirm your faith.

- Provide the class with copies of "The Nicene Creed."
- Read the creed in unison.
- Call attention to the affirmation concerning the church: "We believe in the one, holy, universal, and apostolic church."
- Lead the class in discussing the following questions:

—Does faith "in one, holy, universal, and apostolic church" affirm what is or what ought to be?

—Are denominations a hindrance or a help to realizing "one, holy, universal, and apostolic church?"

—Do Matthew's narratives about Jesus' summoning and sending forth the disciples call the church to a new sense of identity and mission?

(H) Demonstrate the judgment of peace rejected.

Describe a hypothetical case in which two people have experienced alienation.

- Choose two members of the class to portray the alienated persons.
- Seat the persons at opposite sides of the room and invite them to assume positions of obvious distress with their bodies.
- In advance instruct one of the persons to stand up, look tenderly at the other, cross to the other person, reach out, embrace her or him.
- Instruct (again, in advance) the other participant to react angrily, brushing off the embrace and storming from the room.
- Lead the class to discuss what they have witnessed:

—How does the scene reveal the biblical idea of judgment?

—Is judgment imposed?

—Who is the judge?

—What is the difference between experiencing judgment and being judgmental?

—How can we avoid using texts about judgment to condemn others and to protect ourselves?

- Allow sufficient time for class members to discuss the questions above. Offer the following information:

—Matthew emphasized that neither Jesus nor his disciples were to pronounce judgment upon those to whom they were sent. Their message was positive because it announced that the "kingdom of heaven" provided all that was necessary for the total well-being of God's people. Jesus embodied the good news. The Twelve were expected to do the same, revealing in their words and actions the blessings of the Kingdom.

—Although the Twelve were not sent as the agents of God's Final Judgment, how people received them would determine their fate "on the day of judgment." These texts enable us to see that God does not coerce or manipulate persons. God's messengers cannot compel people to accept God. This does not mean, however, that human beings can escape the consequences of their actions. Whether we like it or not, negative consequences result from not accepting God.

—What was the difference between "the lost sheep" and the Twelve? The Twelve were opposed by councils and synagogues, because they imitated Jesus. Persecution was not the goal of their lives; they did not seek martyrdom or enjoy suffering. When they did suffer, however, they did not falter or compromise because their lives were focused on God's mission. The difference between "the twelve" and "the lost sheep" is that no matter what difficulties they encountered, they were never "harassed and helpless."

—These texts help us to see a church that was saved from becoming anxious and self-protective by experiencing that it "was enough" to be like Jesus.

(I) Paraphrase the biblical message.

Rewrite what Jesus said to the Twelve when he sent them out "like sheep into the midst of wolves."

- Distribute pencils and paper to each class member.
- Instruct class members to put Jesus' words, "be wise as serpents and innocent as doves," into contemporary language. Do not use any of the original words.
- Allow sufficient time for class members to paraphrase the biblical text. Invite those who are willing to share them aloud with the class.
- Paraphrasing the text will enable class members to internalize the following insights:

—Ancient metaphors are often difficult for readers today to understand.

—What we think we understand becomes less clear when we attempt to change the wording.

—One of the ways we learn is to accept the fact that we do not understand completely.

—Rewriting a familiar text may bring fresh insight into its meaning.

Dimension 3: What Does the Bible Mean to Us?

(J) Roleplay the need for salvation.

- Select two members of your class to portray a scene in which one person is UNEMPLOYED and the other is a SKILLED EMPLOYEE of an international corporation. Provide each with the information below.
—The employed person volunteers to work in a homeless shelter as a representative of the church. He or she begins a conversation with the unemployed person.
—Many things are discussed, except the issue of unemployment.
—The unemployed person narrates a fruitless attempt to find meaningful work. He or she says poignantly, "The one thing I want more than anything else is a decent job."
- Conclude the roleplay by exploring with the class the following issues:
—Is it possible for people to have meaningful lives without employment?
—Why are some people unemployed?
—What can we do to help provide employment for all our citizens?
—Should the church be actively involved in seeking a solution to unemployment?
—If so, what in the gospel justifies our involvement?
- Allow time for discussion of possible answers.
- Read aloud again Matthew 9:35-38.
—Consider that work often gives human beings dignity and purpose, enabling human beings to have rich and fulfilling lives. The kingdom of heaven is "pie in the sky" unless it offers fullness to those who have been excluded from dignified and purposeful lives because of race, sex, age, religion, or class. Jesus does not condemn our harassed and helpless brothers and sisters. He calls us to become their advocates and servants: "The harvest is plentiful, but the laborers are few; therefore ask the Lord of the harvest to send out laborers into his harvest."
—The authority of the church is expressed best when the church identifies compassionately with "the harassed and helpless" sheep, by assuming the infirmities and diseases of God's children.

(K) Dramatize a reversal.

Prepare a scene that reverses the action of Jesus in our passages.
- Select a member of the class to portray JESUS as a corporate C.E.O.—chief executive officer.
- Choose TWELVE members of the class to apply for positions of leadership in Jesus' corporation.
- Instruct the twelve to present their qualifications to Jesus, hopeful of receiving positions of power in his corporation.
- Ask the interviewees to demand specific benefits.
- Have Jesus instruct those interviewed to put the welfare of the corporation first. Profit is the major concern; work is evaluated by the financial bottom line. Jesus sends those seeking employment into the field on a "practice run." He tells them that if they do not support the corporation, buy its products, and submit to its authority, they are unworthy.
- Conclude the exercise by asking the class members to consider the following:
—Has this reversal actually taken place in our congregation's life?
—Does it underscore the fact that the people of God are always in need of reformation?
- Again, allow the class sufficient time to discuss the roleplay. Class members may have difficulty internalizing that God uses the persecution of faithful witnesses to spread the message of the gospel. This in no way endorses suffering as a good to be sought. Rather it affirms that when the good is sought, it often evokes the opposition of evil forces. In this world, where God is either denied or ignored, the presence of people who affirm God and serve God's will is an affront.
- Invite class members to identify Christians in the past or present whose faithful witness in the face of opposition has exposed them to hatred and persecution.
- List the names of those identified on newsprint or chalkboard.
- Invite class members to identify personal experiences that may have resulted in their being hated for their attempts to faithfully follow Jesus.

If class members have difficulty identifying such experiences, ask if they feel Christians today might not experience persecution because the world has been transformed by the church. Do they feel that modern Christians do not experience persecution because the church has conformed to the world?

(L) Memorize a key verse.

Memorize a key verse as one technique for experiencing what it means to be the reformed people of God. Matthew wanted the church at Antioch to experience the reforming presence of Jesus through his teaching. Today we need that same presence; we often lack it because we do not hear and ponder the words of Jesus.
- Memorize Matthew 10:24-25.
- Plan to use these memorized verses at the beginning of the next class session. Be alert for opportunities throughout the remainder of these lessons to give the class an opportunity to quote these verses.

Additional Bible Helps

A key word in this lesson is *authority*. "Then Jesus summoned his twelve disciples and gave them authority over unclean spirits, to cast them out, and to cure every disease and every sickness" (10:1). Clearly the disciples did not derive their authority from their office or rank but from their relationship to Jesus. Moreover they had no claim on authority; it was given to them.

The tendency in the modern church to understand authority as restricted to certain people (for example, church professionals) because of their office is questionable. A similar tendency in our church today is for persons to claim that they have a right to authority because of their achievements, again contrary to the spirit of these texts.

The word *authority* in this context suggests an authentic, inner power that was exercised because of one's relationship to the ultimate source of power. Jesus had authentic, inner power because of his obedient relationship to God, the ultimate source of power. Jesus participated in God's power by being the agent of God's love in the world. The disciples were summoned by the authority of God's love in Jesus and sent by that authority to be authoritative agents of God's love for the world. That authority could not coerce or manipulate people's response. Only by receiving it freely and giving it freely could it be exercised as authentic, inner power.

The Twelve were not sent by Jesus to assume rank, status, prestige, or privilege in the world but to be servants of the Kingdom. The sign that they participated wholly in the ultimate power of God was that they rejected the rewards of the world, accepting instead the rewards of God (6:1-21). Instead of striving for the pomp and circumstance of the world, it was enough for the disciples to be like their teacher—even to be maligned as Jesus was maligned.

There are some who argue that the followers mentioned in these texts are exclusively the twelve disciples of Jesus, the inner core of his community. Consider another possibility. *Twelve* may be a symbolic number used by Matthew to express the unity, holiness, and universality of the church. The authority given by Jesus to the Twelve is the authority given by Jesus to all Christians. We are set apart for God's service, which is not restricted by historic or geographic limitations. Today we are summoned by Jesus into a community founded upon the love of God. Today we are sent by Jesus to be agents of God's love in the world. We will not be called to perform the same function. Whatever our function, however, it must be validated by the authority to minister, to serve. We know we have the authority, authentic inner power, when we hear and do the words of Jesus.

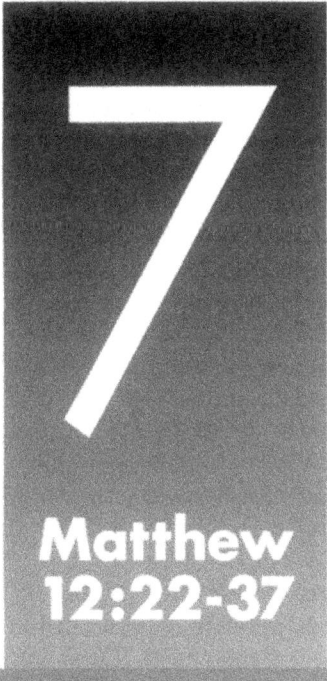

7. The Ministry of Jesus the Messiah Rejected: Blasphemy Against the Holy Spirit

Matthew 12:22-37

LEARNING MENU

This lesson contains two stern warnings about the ultimate seriousness of rejecting the ministry of Jesus: Matthew 12:31-32 and 12:36-37. These sayings of Jesus are often used out of context to make cruel judgments about other people, especially those whom we do not understand and whose actions threaten us. Emphasize the fact that Jesus' warnings were motivated by a desire to make them want to receive his words and deeds.

Keeping in mind the ways in which your class members learn best as well as their needs and interests, choose at least one learning segment from each of the three Dimensions.

Dimension 1: What Does the Bible Say?

Throughout this entire section, which begins at 9:35 and concludes at 13:53, Jesus taught his disciples about the ministry that he has called them and equipped them to perform. One of the issues they confronted was the resistance they encountered and how they would cope with that resistance. Matthew used these texts to help the church learn how to deal with rejection. They are relevant for us as we experience rejection of our own ministry today.

One of the knee-jerk reactions to evil is to resist by responding in kind. Thus evil begets evil, and the vicious cycle of violence is perpetuated. Matthew reminds us that Jesus broke the cycle of violence by refusing to "wrangle or cry aloud" (12:19). He raised neither his voice nor his hand in anger because he was not motivated by the spirit of revenge but by the Spirit of mercy. He was faithful to his message of justice and persistent in his ministry of bringing good out of the treasure of his heart. Since his heart overflowed with treasure, there was no room for hatred, violence, or vengeance. He saved his people from their sins by showing them the compassion of God in his words and deeds.

(A) Read the text dramatically.

As in earlier sessions, read today's text dramatically.
- You will need to choose the following roles from among your class members: JESUS, NARRATOR, THE CROWD, and a PHARISEE.

(B) Answer the questions from the study book.

- Discuss class members' reflections to the questions raised in the study book. Note responses on either chalkboard or newsprint.
  Possible answers to these questions are

1. Jesus' exorcisms were seen as evidence of having power over evil.

2. Satan's power was overcome by the power of one stronger—Jesus. To the Pharisees it looked like an "insider's job." That is, they accused Jesus of being a cohort of Satan.

3. Blasphemy involved dishonoring God's name. In this case, Jesus was able to forgive sins because he was divine. The rejection of his divine ministry was blasphemy.

4. The heart was considered the region of thought, intention, and moral disposition.

(C) Discuss violence.

- Divide the class into three groups. Then say, "Someone has said 'violence is as American as apple pie.'" In each group discuss whether you believe this statement is true.
—Ask *group one* to identify instances where violence is advocated as a solution to evil on TV or in the media.
—Ask *group two* to identify instances of this action happening in the news media.
—Instruct *group three* to focus attention upon the perception that weapons are purchased by private citizens to protect themselves against evil.
- Each group should designate a reporter to share its perceptions when the class reassembles. Record the results on chalkboard or newsprint.
- Lead the class in a consideration of the following questions:
—Does the use of violent language encourage the use of violent action?
—Is it easier to arouse anger against something than to evoke commitment to something?
—Does the endorsement of violent solutions to evil tend to endorse evil itself?
—Can we glorify violent responses to evil without rejecting the ministry of Jesus?

Dimension 2: What Does the Bible Mean?

This lesson confronts us with one of the most perplexing aspects of the ministry of Jesus. There is no recorded instance of his attacking others in his words or deeds, yet his message and his actions caused some of the leaders of the Jewish religious establishment to conspire to kill him. One of the questions this lesson raises and is raised throughout the Gospel of Matthew is this: Why did Jesus' nonviolent ministry meet with a violent reaction?

The Pharisees exercised authority over others. Jesus posed a threat to their special privilege because he ministered to all the people as one whose authority was from God. His authority was not revealed in his special privilege but in his gentle and humble service.

The people were attracted to him. They began to see the difference between Jesus and the Pharisees. They wondered if he might not be the promised Messiah, the Son of David, who would bring God's salvation to them. The Pharisees rejected his ministry because they were jealous of his popularity with the people. They were afraid that his ministry would liberate the people from their control.

Another reason the Pharisees found to reject Jesus was his power. Since Jesus was able to deliver people from evil, the Pharisees concluded that it was because he himself was a participant in the power structure of evil. His power was not different from the forces of evil, but the fact that evil was submissive to him indicated to them that he was a part of the realm of evil (12:24). By taking this attitude toward Jesus' ministry, the Pharisees were able to acknowledge the unusual power exercised by Jesus and at the same time to oppose it as evil.

Jesus countered the charge of the Pharisees by appealing to common sense. It was completely illogical to argue that evil could cast out evil or overthrow evil. The reason that Jesus was able to cast out demons was his reliance upon a superior power, the Spirit of God. Jesus explained the power of his ministry in his reply to the accusation of the Pharisees in 12:28-29.

Jesus' ministry challenged the Pharisees' traditional understanding of power. True power was the power of God. God's power as revealed in the ministry of Jesus was the power to serve others, not the power of status and special privilege. Jesus called the Pharisees to repent, to turn from their false understanding of power and to accept the true meaning of power as equipment for service.

In the presence of Jesus, the Pharisees and all the people were required to make a clear choice. Either they would accept the kingdom of God in their midst and choose to live under its power or they would reject the kingdom of God and choose to live under the power of evil. The words of Jesus in 12:30 clarified the issue sharply.

(D) Roleplay the conflict.

- Choose three members of the class to play JESUS, a BLIND AND MUTE PERSON, and a PHARISEE.
- Set the blind and mute person at center stage.
- Jesus enters, lays his hands upon the afflicted person, and the blind and mute person is healed.
- The Pharisee, standing to one side watching Jesus' action, now comes forward and declares, "It is only by Beelzebul, the ruler of the demons, that this fellow casts out the demons."
- Jesus responds to the Pharisee, "Every kingdom divided against itself is laid waste, and no city or house divided against itself will stand. If Satan casts out Satan, he is divided against himself; how then will his kingdom stand? If I cast out demons by Beelzebul, by whom do

your own exorcists cast them out? Therefore they will be your judges. But if it is by the Spirit of God that I cast out demons, then the kingdom of God has come to you. Or how can one enter a strong man's house and plunder his property, without first tying up the strong man? Then indeed the house may be plundered. Whoever is not with me is against me, and whoever does not gather with me scatters."

- Lead the class in a discussion of the following issues:
— How did this scene call the Pharisees to repentance?
— What would repentance mean for the Pharisee?
— What are the evidences of evil in the drama?
— How does Jesus respond to evil?

Jesus' teaching about the terrible consequences of blasphemy against the Holy Spirit was reported by Matthew in its context: do not damn those who rejected Jesus but make them want to be with Jesus and to join him in his ministry of mercy. Jesus' clear and forceful language was directed to those who were blind to the truth and unable to become witnesses to that truth.

As long as the Pharisees were possessed by the evil in their hearts, they were doomed to be blind and mute. Jesus' ministry to them began with their condition so that they would be able to recognize the truth about themselves and be cured. The Final Judgment had already come upon them, however, because Jesus could not give them what they did not recognize as their need.

Jesus was not passive in the face of those who spoke evil against him. He engaged them directly and showed the depth of his compassion for them by speaking the truth. He cared for them enough to tell them the truth about themselves even if that truth might harden their resolve to destroy him.

When the Pharisees began to conspire to kill him, Jesus did not forsake his vocation and respond to them with hate. He was consistently and persistently the agent of God's mercy not only to those who followed him but also to those who rejected him. Jesus continued to offer them the forgiveness of God, but he could not force them to accept it. The Final Judgment was simply the fact that their desire to do harm to another person made it impossible for them to receive forgiveness "either in this age or in the age to come" (32).

(E) Dramatize how we are judged.

- Choose two members of the class to act out a scene that illustrates how we cannot receive what we do not want.
- In this scene, two people become engaged in a bitter dispute. They speak evil of one another and threaten to do one another harm. They hurl accusations at one another but never examine their own attitudes and actions. It soon becomes clear that they do not want reconciliation, mercy, or justice. What they really want is vindication, revenge, and victory. What they do not want they cannot receive.
- Lead the class in exploring these questions:
— How does this scene shed light on Jesus' teaching about blasphemy against the Holy Spirit?
— How does the Holy Spirit work in our lives today?
— Is it possible to hate evil without also hating the people who do evil things?
— How does Jesus' teaching and ministry help us to see our own needs and to be open to God's gracious gifts?

In this text Jesus spoke directly to those who rejected his ministry. His compassion for them was expressed by his caring enough to speak directly to them. He did not talk about them to others. He was free in taking this action because his trust in God delivered him from anxiety for his own life. It freed him to lose his life in service for others, even when the others sought to destroy him.

Since Jesus desired the kingdom of God more than anything else, he was empowered by that desire to speak and act as an agent of God's will on earth. He believed that the power of good was superior to the power of evil. His commitment to good was a concrete decision to love his enemies so that they would be transformed by his love into faithful followers.

(F) Discuss ways to offer hope.

Present the following situation to the group. A prominent and respected member of a local congregation has become involved in a financial scandal. She or he has been indicted, convicted, and sentenced to prison. The immediate response of many people in the congregation is to gossip to each other *about* her or him. Someone who has been mistreated by the person and suffered loss because of the crime seeks out the criminal, speaks directly about the crime, offers understanding and support, and affirms faith in a new beginning.

- Lead the class in a discussion of the following concerns:
— Do we talk *about* other people because we decide they are hopeless?
— Do we judge others as hopeless because we want to protect ourselves from involvement in their struggles?
— Might speaking directly *to* people as they struggle indicate that we care for them and want to help them?
— Can we believe in the good news of the Kingdom and simultaneously treat another person as hopeless?

Dimension 3: What Does the Bible Mean to Us?

One of the most tragic misuses of this Scripture has been its use in supporting anti-Semitic attitudes and actions. It is important to note that not all Pharisees and not all Jews rejected the ministry of Jesus. Jesus himself was a faithful

Jew as were the majority of those who became his disciples. Quite likely when Matthew wrote his Gospel around 85 C.E. he used this rejection of Jesus' ministry to warn the church itself of the Pharisaic attitude. If this idea is true, then these texts are not about "them" but about "us." They should be read against the background of Jesus' warning about misusing Scripture to condemn and exclude others (5:21-48). They are to be used as a mirror for recognizing our own failures (7:1-5).

It is not likely that we will experience this lesson as a call to repentance by focusing upon the evil done by those who rejected Jesus. The texts do not proclaim evil but rather they present Jesus as the one in whose words and deeds the kingdom of God has come. He is the major actor and the principal speaker.

In the light of his love we see our own hatred. His mercy brings to light our failure to be merciful. His courage highlights our cowardice. His giving of himself illuminates our rejection of his gifts. His hope challenges our despair. His faithfulness shames our betrayal. These texts bring us into the presence of the kingdom of God when our heightened awareness of Jesus' goodness leaves us with this command: "You must change your life."

Repentance is a possibility now, even for Pharisees, even for us, because God is at work in us curing our blindness and muteness. God wants us to see the good news of the Kingdom and make it known. God's abiding presence through the Holy Spirit is the precondition of our being with God and sharing in God's ministry. The more we realize God's presence in these texts, the more we are drawn to and transformed by them.

(G) Create images of goodness.

- Provide the class with modeling clay, crayons, pencils, and paper.
- Encourage class members to imagine Jesus' presence with them in a crisis. Then ask them to portray his goodness by forming images with the clay, drawing pictures with the crayons, or writing a poem.
- When class members have finished their artistic interpretations, encourage them to share their creations.
- Conclude the exercise by leading the class to explore the following:

—What are the points of contact between the good we see in Jesus and the good in our own lives?

—How do images of the good in Jesus make us aware of evil in us and in our society?

—How do the images of Jesus' goodness release positive forces for good in your own life?

—How do images of Jesus' goodness make you want to change your life?

The stern warnings about our accountability in these texts are not negative but positive. They reveal to us the fact that although God honors our freedom and does not override our choices, we are not deserted by God when we reject God's will for our lives. God's faithfulness in loving us means that God does not deal with us as if we did not matter and as if our choices had no final significance. The words and deeds of Jesus remind us of the truth about ourselves, cure us of our bondage to lies, and give us courage to speak the truth.

Today the Spirit of God is present in our personal and corporate experience, reminding us of our accountability for the choices we make. To the extent that we have carelessly and ruthlessly abused God's good creation, we have reaped the consequences of eroded fields, polluted streams, ruined landscapes, blighted communities, and desperate people. It is not that we have not heard voices of truth telling us about the consequences of unbridled greed and unrestrained consumption, but rather that we have dismissed these voices as agents of Beelzebul. We have blasphemed against the Holy Spirit, and so long as we are blind and mute, we will not be forgiven in this age or the age to come. This does not mean that God has left us to destroy ourselves. It simply means that not even God can force us to receive what we do not desire.

(H) Discuss denial of addiction.

One of the common reactions of addicted persons is denial. As long as a person is in denial, there is no possibility of either desiring or receiving help. Point out that there are evidences that this is an addictive society.

- Help the class to identify such addictions as the acceptance of violence, the promotion of competition, the desire for independence, the quest for pleasure, and so forth. The more "respectable" an addiction is, the more difficult it is to identify and the more entrenched it becomes as a normal part of life.
- Lead the class to explore this subject by raising the following questions:

—What are the evidences of addictions in our lives?

—Why do we seek to discredit people who speak about our addictions?

- Summarize the following information.

One of the cruelest things we say to ourselves or to others is, "If you just wanted to be better, you could be better." It is saying to those in need that we have no responsibility for them and that they can only get help from within themselves. This is the basic problem with all self-help approaches to human need. They shut people off from resources beyond themselves, often leaving them helpless and hopeless. The good news of the Kingdom is radically different. Our situation of need has already been radically changed by God's action in Jesus. God is not only *with* us. God is unconditionally *for* us. The basic vocation of Jesus is to reveal this truth about God to people so that they will desire God with all their being and be transformed by the good treasure of their heart.

The good news of the Kingdom is unconditional. It does not begin with "*If* you just wanted to be better," but rather it begins with "*Since* God is with you in Jesus, you can be perfect in love even as God is perfect."

(I) Reflect on Jesus' ministry.

Perhaps the most important resource available to you as you teach is the class itself. Your teaching will become more rewarding for you and for the class as you are able to get in touch with this resource and to rely upon it.

- Invite the class to share how they have experienced changes because of the good news of Jesus' ministry.
- Affirm the variety of experiences by pointing out how we are enriched by hearing other people's stories.
- Encourage others to participate by telling your own story.
- Say a prayer of gratitude for experiences of the transforming love of God in Jesus.

Additional Bible Helps

The task of studying Matthew in thirteen lessons is overwhelming. Therefore, it is important to keep in mind that each lesson is intended to be introductory rather than exhaustive. The hope is that the cumulative effect of the lessons will inspire the class to continue their study and will give them some skills and techniques which will help them to be better students of the Bible. You can encourage this process by referring to related passages in the course of your development of a particular lesson. The following comments are illustrative of this technique.

One of the presuppositions of Jesus' teaching is that it is not enough to be against evil to be victorious over evil. We have evidence to support this idea in our own experience. For example, the "war on crime," which is one of the clichés of political candidates, stirs emotions, hardens public opinion against criminals, and leads to harsh sentences of convicted criminals. The concentration of energy and resources upon apprehending and punishing criminals often is not accompanied by a clear commitment to programs that create jobs, provide education, establish justice, and promote community. The result is that crime is not overcome because the social conditions and personal attitudes that are the breeding ground of crime are neither recognized nor addressed.

Perhaps we have been unable to rid our streets of violent crime and to make our communities peaceful because we have ignored the following words of Jesus: "When the unclean spirit has gone out of a person, it wanders through waterless regions looking for a resting place, but it finds none. Then it says, 'I will return to my house from which I came.' When it comes, it finds it empty, swept, and put in order. Then it goes and brings along seven other spirits more evil than itself, and they enter and live there; and the last state of that person is worse than the first. So will it be also with this evil generation" (12:43-45).

The reference to "this evil generation" supports the conclusion that Jesus was not only speaking to individuals but to communities. His words apply to our contemporary "war on crime." They remind us that a "house" or community "empty, swept, and put in order" by locking criminals away out of sight is a vacuum of values and commitment that makes our last state worse than the first.

Matthew 12:43-45 is an integral part of Jesus' instruction to his disciples about the ministry that he has called and equipped them to perform. Consider this text in your lesson plan by referring to it in the course of your development of 12:22-37. A better approach would be to assign it to a member of the class and at the appropriate time call for a report on its meaning and application. This not only gives a member of the class an opportunity to take responsibility for the learning process, it also demonstrates how A Daily Bible Journey Plan contains material relevant for the Scripture considered in a particular lesson.

Using this technique will encourage the class to look for connecting links in Scripture and to rely upon those links as clues to interpretation and application. Reference to 12:43-45 may help you to interpret repentance as basically a positive turning toward the goodness of God instead of a negative turning away from evil.

The weakness of the negative approach is that it ignores the fact that to be fully human we have to give ourselves to something *greater than ourselves*. It is simply not enough for us to be "empty, swept, and put in order." An essential element of Jesus' call to repentance is his calling us to share in his meaningful work. We are not really delivered from evil until we accept our vocation and give fully to it. One of the practical consequences of this approach is that each time we hear the good news of the Kingdom, our vocation as the children of God is clarified and intensified.

When we understand repentance as a positive turning toward God so that the emptiness of our hearts is filled by the kingdom of God, then we become aware of repentance as a continuing experience of Jesus' followers. Repentance, then, is not something that we did long ago when we chose to follow Jesus. It is the centering of our life in the goodness of God. This centering is never finished because Jesus always comes to us with a new revelation of God's gifts. Our receiving them depends upon our seeking them with all our heart.

8 — The Ministry of Jesus the Messiah Misunderstood: The Necessity of the Cross

Matthew 16:13-28

LEARNING MENU

Remind the class that Jesus continues to be present with us as the risen Lord who, through the power of the Holy Spirit, continually is revealing himself more fully to us.

Choose at least one learning segment from each of the three Dimensions.

Dimension 1: What Does the Bible Say?

(A) Prepare a worship center.

- Before class members arrive, prepare a visual on an altar or low table in the classroom. Since today's lesson focuses on the foundation of the church, gather several different shapes and sizes of rocks. Arrange these attractively on the table. Intersperse live, green plants among the rocks. Place an open Bible in the visual.

(B) Make a nametag.

- As members arrive, ask each to make a nametag.
- Provide adhesive nametags that can be purchased in most office stores OR provide scraps of construction paper and straight pins. Provide markers and several books that feature meanings of first names. (Check your local public or church library. Parents-to-be or parents of young children also may own such books.)
- Instruct class members to write the meaning of their first name on their tag (for instance, instead of "Debra," write "Bee").
- Invite a pianist to play the hymn "The Church's One Foundation," or invite a class member to sing this hymn, as class members walk around the room silently reading each other's nametags.

(C) Answer the questions from the study book.

As class members arrive, ask them to turn to the questions on page 60 in the study book. Class members who have already considered answers to the questions may benefit from discussing their responses with another person.

Possible answers to these questions are

1. Some people compared Jesus to other "forerunners" of the Messiah—Elijah, Jeremiah, or one of the other prophets. Peter answered on behalf of the Twelve that Jesus was the Messiah.

2. Jesus said that Peter would be the foundation in building the church against which evil would not be ultimately effective.

3. Jesus consistently sought to repress sensational reports. (See also Mark 8:30.)

4. The idea that the Son of man would suffer was a complete contradiction of Jewish messianic expectations. Peter attempted to coerce Jesus to "live into" commonly held understandings of the Messiah.

One way to help your class engage this lesson in a fresh way is to call its attention to the lesson's confrontational nature. Jesus took the initiative by raising a question about his identity. It seems that the Twelve did not want to address their understanding of Jesus' identity. They seemed to be content to avoid the issue by simply reporting what others thought. Jesus was determined to force them to answer the question for themselves. Creating an atmosphere of tension, he pressed the Twelve with the question, "But who do you say that I am?"

At one level, Peter's response to Jesus reflected what had been revealed to him and the other disciples by God. "You are the Messiah, the Son of the living God" acknowledged Jesus' special relationship to God. Peter could affirm that relationship with certainty and deep commitment. These words were the "rock" upon which Jesus would build his church. They summarized the essence of the good news of the Kingdom (16:18). They were words that enabled the *church* to assault evil, just as Jesus was able to *overcome* evil (16:18).

Jesus could not approve this answer unconditionally, however, because it did not include the cross as the inevitable result of his special relationship to God. Therefore, Jesus "sternly ordered the disciples not to tell anyone that he was the Messiah" (16:20).

The remainder of the lesson hinges upon what Jesus showed his disciples about his cross. Until Peter's misunderstanding about that was corrected, the disciples had no distinctive message and no authoritative mission. The dialogue between Jesus and Peter made this point dramatically clear. When Jesus showed his disciples "that he must go to Jerusalem and undergo great suffering at the hands of the elders and chief priests and scribes, and be killed, and on the third day be raised" (16:21), he set off a heated exchange with Peter. The conflict was face-to-face and direct. Peter rebuked Jesus in the strongest possible language, "God forbid it, Lord! This must never happen to you" (16:22). Jesus replied, "Get behind me, Satan! You are a stumbling block to me; for you are setting your mind not on divine things but on human things" (16:23). One might describe the exchange as a verbal head-on collision between two radically opposed positions; there was no possibility of compromise or arbitration.

(D) Read the Scripture dramatically.

- Introduce the dramatic presentation of Matthew 16:13-28 by analyzing the meaning of the word *rebuke* used in the text. In this context, *rebuke* means "to admonish or charge sharply." Invite class members to watch for moments of rebuke as they watch or participate in the presentation.
- Select one member of the class to be the NARRATOR, one to be JESUS, one to be PETER, and the others to be the ELEVEN DISCIPLES.
- Direct the narrator to stand off-stage and read all the material that is not in quotation marks.
- As the narrator reads, class members dramatizing Peter and Jesus walk along, with the other disciples following.
- Suddenly, Jesus stops and asks his question about his identity."Who do people say that the Son of Man is?"
- The disciples answer in chorus:"Some say John the Baptist, but others Elijah, and still others Jeremiah or one of the prophets."
- Focus the rest of the dialogue between Jesus and Peter, using the storyline presented in verses 15-23. The disciples should remain within earshot. Jesus will directly address the disciples at points.
- Conclude the exercise. Divide the class into groups of three. Invite groups to consider the following questions:
—What did you hear that was new?
—How would you describe what you saw?
—How do you feel about the experience?
—What special relevance do your new insights have for your own relationship to Jesus?

Dimension 2: What Does the Bible Mean?

Share the following information:

One of the most complicated technical problems in New Testament scholarship is Jesus' use of the term *Son of man* to refer to himself. In Matthew, as well as in Mark and Luke, he used it in three different ways:
—to refer to his ministry and his authority on earth (8:20);
—to predict his suffering and death (17:22-23);
—to speak of his return in glory as the judge of the end time (25:31).

In this lesson Jesus uses "Son of Man" to refer to his earthly ministry of humble service (16:13) and to his return as the glorious ruler and judge of the end time (16:27-28). The point is that Jesus who is present *now* as the gentle and humble servant and who is subject to the judgment of people *will be revealed at the end time* as the judge who subjects all people to his judgment. What people say and do about the revelation of the Kingdom will determine their future standing in his reign.

This section addresses a theme announced earlier by Jesus in 10:32-33. The text clarifies the relationship between a right understanding of Jesus and a right understanding of the church. Peter and the disciples did not arrive at a right definition of their life together as the church except in the context of their understanding of Jesus. Just as Jesus was defined by his special relationship to God, "You are the Messiah, the Son of the living God" (16:16), so the church was defined by its special relationship to God, revealed in Jesus. The blessedness of the church was the fact that it was created by that relationship and sustained by it. Peter, as the representative of the whole church, was no longer to be identified by his human lineage, "son of Jonah," but as "Peter," a new person transformed by the blessedness of the good news of the Kingdom. He was the "rock" upon which Jesus would build his church. His new life manifested "the church's one foundation," the revelation of the kingdom of God in the words and deeds of Jesus.

This doctrine of the church, ecclesiology, arises from the doctrine of "Christology." Note that this is Matthew's first use of the word *church* (in Greek, *ecclessia*). Peter, the disciples, and Matthew's community in Antioch would not understand their life together in the church unless they understood their life together with Jesus as the revelation of the good news of the Kingdom. The question was not how the church understood *itself*, but how the church understood *Jesus*. If the primary relationship was wrong then the secondary relationship would be wrong also. Matthew seemed to be saying to the church at Antioch that preoccupation with leadership roles in the church, anxiety about church order, and debates about church doctrine would be demonic unless they were informed by a right relationship to "Jesus the Messiah, the Son of the living God."

(E) Sing hymns.

- Provide hymnals containing the hymn, "The Church's One Foundation." If hymnals are not available, line out the stanzas so that members may sing it.
- Invite a musician to lead the class in singing the hymn.
- Silently consider the text of the hymn.
- Discuss the meaning of the hymn by raising the following questions:
—What are the similarities between the hymn and Matthew 16:13-28?
—What are the differences?
—In what ways does study of the Scripture lesson deepen understanding of the hymn?
—In what ways does singing the hymn deepen understanding of the Scripture lesson?
- Share the following information:
—There is tension in the text between Jesus' approval of Peter's affirmation and his stern order that the disciples remain silent about his messiahship. Matthew may have used this tradition to warn the church of Antioch that disciples could use the right words about Jesus without understanding those words correctly. It was possible to say that Jesus was the Christ and understand him as a nationalistic leader who would use military might to restore the kingdom of David. It was also possible to say that Jesus was the Son of the living God and understand him as a miracle worker who would use his miraculous power to protect himself and destroy his enemies. It was possible to say the right words and at the same time set one's mind on "human things." Each of these possibilities was ultimately realized in the church.
—The right words about Jesus always had to be corrected and reformed by what Jesus showed his disciples about the connection between his vocation and his relationship to God. "From that time on" (21) emphasized the need for the church's confession to always be interpreted by the Passion. That need was never satisfied by words. It had to be fulfilled by Jesus giving himself in service and continued in the church responding in service. Just as Jesus had to show them the cross as the heart of his vocation, so they had to show him the cross at the heart of their affirmation. To do God's will Jesus had to deny himself to find himself. The disciples were not above their teacher, nor greater than their master (10:16-25). If they wanted to be his followers, they had to deny themselves and take up their cross and follow him.
—In a sense what Peter said to Jesus in response to the necessity of the cross was an attempt to manipulate Jesus to conform to popular understandings about the Messiah, instead of allowing those understandings to be transformed by the cross. Jesus resisted Peter. He recognized the temptation to use God for his own purpose instead of allowing God to use him for God's purposes. The choice was clear and decisive!

(F) Roleplay a biblical scene.

- Invite a class member to roleplay the part of JESUS in the text.
- Cast all other class members as DISCIPLES.
- Jesus asks the disciples, "Who do people say that the Son of Man is?"

The disciples respond in chorus: "Some say John the Baptist, but others Elijah, and still others Jeremiah or one of the prophets."

Jesus asks, "But who do you say that I am?"

The disciples again chorus: "You are the Messiah, the Son of the living God."

Jesus sternly orders them, "Be silent! Do not tell anyone that I am the Messiah."

- Give the class time to reflect on this dramatic exchange. Help members to glean the meaning of the passage for themselves by raising the following issues:
—Are these the right words to say about Jesus?
—Why or why not?
—What are some other right words to affirm Jesus?
—Does our behavior ever reflect that we use the right

words to conceal the fact that we have not really followed Jesus?
— How does Jesus' showing us his cross correct our profession?
— Is it possible to follow Jesus without ever having said the right words about him?
• Share the following information.
— Matthew indicated that the church at Antioch was prosperous. For example, Jesus' blessing on "the poor" in Luke 6:20 is changed to a blessing on "the poor in spirit" in Matthew 5:3. Luke had Jesus tell a parable about "minas" in 19:11-27; however, in Matthew 25:14-30 Jesus told the parable about "talents." (A talent was worth at least fifty times as much as a mina.) Matthew specifically identified Joseph of Arimathea as "a rich man," but in Mark and Luke he was simply a "member of the council." Matthew mentioned "silver," "gold," and "talent" twenty-eight times. Mark mentioned "silver" once; Luke made four referencess. The church at Antioch was probably accustomed to wealth and subject to the peculiar temptations of affluence.
— Against the background of a prosperous Christian church, the rhetorical questions of Jesus in 16:26 were especially pointed. "For what will it profit them if they gain the whole world but forfeit their life? Or what will they give in return for their life?" The implied answer to both questions was, "Nothing." The text is about one's allegiance to God revealed in Jesus, about setting one's mind on divine rather than human things, about one's relationship to God, about taking up the cross and following Jesus. One would be judged by what one did on earth, including how one used one's wealth. If it were used to protect only one's self and save one's life, one would be repaid in death. If wealth was used to serve others, one would be repaid in life. In the Last Judgment, the appearance of wealth and the security of possessions would avail nothing. "For the Son of Man is to come with his angels in the glory of his Father, and then he will repay everyone for what has been done" (27).

(G) Read and discuss the parable of the talents.

• Read the parable in Matthew 25:14-30.
• Divide the class into three groups: the FIVE-TALENT GROUP, the TWO-TALENT GROUP, and THE ONE-TALENT GROUP.
• Assign each group the task of discussing this question, Upon what was the master's judgment of his slaves based when he returned and required them to settle accounts with him?
• Record the answers on newsprint or chalkboard.
• Discuss the results by posing the following questions:
— What is the relationship between affirming Jesus as the Messiah, the Son of the living God, and stewardship?

— Do you think stewardship is a matter of setting one's mind on divine things instead of human things?
— Does affluence pose special temptations to those who want to follow Jesus?

Dimension 3: What Does the Bible Mean to Us?

As Christians we are required to reaffirm our faith and meet the special challenges of our changing situation. Openness is required. Our claims to know Jesus may keep us from entering into new experiences of following him on the way that leads to life.

For instance, Jesus' words to Peter have a past, a present, and future reference: "Blessed are you [present tense], Simon son of Jonah! For flesh and blood has not revealed [past tense] this to you, but my Father in heaven. And I tell you [present tense], you are Peter, and on this rock I will build [future tense] my church, and the gates of Hades will not [future tense] prevail against it" (16:17-18). One conclusion we can draw is that the church has a rather unfinished relationship with Jesus. It has a past, a present, and a promise to bring together the action of God in Jesus as the future unfolds. The church must claim the promises of God by recommitting to God's purpose as revealed in Jesus.

(H) Reflect on a friendship analogy.

• Use an analogy of friendship to experience why the church is always unfinished.
• Choose two class members to demonstrate the dynamics of friendship. Two friends discuss an issue about which they have strong convictions.
• As the conversation progresses, one of the friends becomes quiet. Then the quiet friend says, "I thought I knew how you stood on this issue, but now I see that I completely misunderstood you."
• The second friend says, "No. You were right. Over the course of time, however, I have changed. I have been forced to change in light of new information and new circumstances."
• Allow the class time to reflect on the exchange.
• Guide the class to discuss the exchange by posing the following questions:
— Do we often "pigeonhole" friends because we presume we know them?
— Does the presumption that we know an individual cause us to take the person for granted and stop listening to what is said?
— Does friendship need to be updated and renewed in light of current experiences?
— Is the analogy of human friendship useful as we try to

understand the dynamics of our relationship to God as revealed in Jesus Christ?

The text challenges us to consider that all our understandings about Jesus are limited by our perspective. Therefore, we must never be content with our current knowledge of Jesus. Be open and responsive to new revelations through study, prayer, worship, and fellowship with other believers.

(I) Reflect on the cross of Jesus.

- Add a cross to your visual of rocks and plants.
- Encourage class members to sit quietly and reflect on Jesus' self-giving love.
- As class members feel able, invite them to place their nametag (created earlier and worn in the class session) in the worship visual.
- Invite small groups of three to discuss what the cross shows them about God, about Jesus, about themselves, and about the world.
- Close by singing the hymn "When I Survey the Wondrous Cross" or another hymn about the cross.
- The lesson began with a question about words but it climaxes with an emphasis on deeds. Words about Jesus are important. They express the allegiance of the heart, the inner disposition, so that the object of affection becomes the ruler of one's action. Words that are not confirmed by deeds are hypocritical. Likewise, deeds that do not reveal the allegiance of the heart quickly fade away. People are driven by what they want. The church will experience the same judgment: "He [the glorious Son of man] will repay everyone for what has been done" (16:27). Those "who deny themselves and take up their cross and follow" Jesus will receive life; but those who indulge themselves, avoid their cross, and go their own way will receive death. The Final Judgment is not something an angry God does to us. It is what we do to ourselves. We get what we want.

Additional Bible Helps

A key word in this lesson is *cross*. It is used in 16:24 to suggest it had already become a symbol for the life of disciples: "If any want to become my followers, let them deny themselves and take up their cross and follow me" (16:24). This meaning is reflected in 10:38 where it clearly refers to discipleship: "Whoever does not take up the cross and follow me is not worthy of me." The cross was a requirement for any who wanted to be disciples of Jesus.

Before the cross was interpreted as an essential requirement of discipleship, it had been given its unique meaning by the passion of Jesus. The starting point for understanding the cross as a requirement of discipleship is Jesus' showing "his disciples that he must go to Jerusalem and undergo great suffering at the hands of the elders and chief priests and scribes, and be killed, and on the third day be raised" (16:21). The prediction of his Passion in 17:22-23 and 20:18-19 reinforced this idea. These passages provided the framework for the Passion narrative itself and are expanded and interpreted by the report of Jesus' trial, persecution, crucifixion, and resurrection. We know the meaning of the cross. The cross for Jesus was not a tragedy that occurred at the end of his life. It was his chosen way of life, his vocation.

We can recover something of the true meaning of the cross by recalling certain historical facts. Crucifixion was a cruel and excruciating form of execution adapted by the Romans as a punishment for slaves, noncitizens, and occasionally for citizens guilty of treason. Suffering might last for days, death being preceded by thirst, high fever, pain, and convulsions. Occasionally the executioners hastened death by breaking the victim's bones. One's humiliation was heightened by flogging or being forced to carry the cross to the execution site.

Although Jesus was tried and condemned as a common criminal, clearly he was innocent. His "cross," then, was Emmanuel, "God with us" in our sin. He saved us from sin by becoming one with us out of obedience to God. His suffering, rejection, and death were not accidents of his human condition but the consequence of his special relationship to God.

The cross borne by Jesus' followers is not to be equated with suffering such human frailties as disease. To do so trivializes the gospel. We truly experience the cross only when we deny ourselves, accept our vocation as disciples, and follow Jesus. Followers must willingly accept the task of "being Christian on purpose."

9

The Ministry of Jesus the Messiah Denied: The Grief of Self-Reliance

Matthew 19:13-30

LEARNING MENU

As we study this lesson, we should strive to keep before us the grief that we experience when we follow the example of the young man who "went away grieving, for he had many possessions" (22) and the reward that we experience when we follow the example of Jesus.

Keeping in mind the ways in which your class members learn best as well as their needs and interests, choose at least one learning segment from each of the three Dimensions.

Dimension 1:
What Does the Bible Say?

The lesson consists of four dramatic, interconnected episodes. The *first episode* depicts the crisis created when the disciples rebuked those who were bringing the little children to Jesus. The tension in the action occurred when Jesus' words and deeds contradicted the disciples' implied words and deeds. Jesus did not want one of the little ones to be lost. The disciples acted as if they despised the little ones. Their attitude was important, for Jesus said it was "to such as these that the kingdom of heaven belongs" (14). If the disciples did not value the little children, then they could not value the kingdom of heaven.

The *second episode* consists of dialogue between a rich young man and Jesus. The man asked questions, the answers to which he had already anticipated. He sought confirmation of his life from Jesus. Jesus instead confronted him with the poor, who were synonymous with the little children. The poor represented the kingdom of heaven, just as the little children represented the kingdom of heaven. The young man needed the kingdom of heaven more than anything else but he could not receive it as a private possession. He could only receive it in a community of mutual need and mutual service. As long as the young man sought to possess eternal life (the kingdom of heaven) by excluding others, he was destined to lose it. His grief was the sorrow of self-reliance, of valuing possessions more than community, and of wanting treasure on earth more than treasure in heaven. He represents the consequences of would-be disciples despising the little ones.

The *third episode*, dialogue between Jesus and his disciples, picks up and elaborates on the themes developed in the first two: the way of disciples, the way of following Jesus by receiving little children, is radically different from the way of the world. The way of the world was the way of the young man, the way of the rich. The rich represent self-reliance and power, worldly values and rewards. Jesus astounded his disciples when he stated clearly that it was impossible to follow the way of the world and enter the kingdom of God. If the self-reliant and powerful were excluded, then who would be included? The answer was the little children, but not by any mortal power. They would be included by the power of God. The possibility of salvation includes everyone through God's self-giving love in Jesus. We all may become God's little ones.

The *final episode* affirms the reward that awaits ideal disciples. Those persons will follow the way of Jesus. They will receive the little ones on earth. They will be repaid at the Final Judgment. They will get what they *want*. They will be with Jesus (the glorified Son of man) in the authority of his love, and that love will be the standard by which the people of God are judged. Eternal life will be their inheritance. Their reward will be the joy of the little ones who have come home.

(A) Answer the questions in the study book.

- As in previous weeks, spend the moments when class members arrive in discussing their answers to the questions in the study book, page 68.

(B) Dramatize the lesson.

- Produce a four-act drama based on the text.
- In the first act (19:13-15), the actors are JESUS, the PARENTS and their CHILDREN, and the DISCIPLES. Ask actors to portray the children in a way that observers will associate them with the sick, the blind, the lame, the demon possessed, and the poor. Instruct actors to emphasize the contrast between the response of the disciples and Jesus to the little children.
- In the second act (19:16-22), the actors are JESUS and THE RICH YOUNG MAN. One of the key portrayals should be the transformation in the young man from one who is self-assured and confident to one who goes away grieving. Instruct actors to contrast the way the young man interprets the Commandments to exclude others and protect himself and the way Jesus interprets Scripture to include others and to give himself.
- The third act (19:23-26) is a conversation between JESUS and his DISCIPLES. The statements of Jesus explain the meaning of the first two acts. The astonishment of the disciples is one of the major emphases in the third act.
- The final act (19:27-30) features PETER and JESUS.
- At the close of the drama divide the class into four groups. Assign each group one of the following questions:
—What did Jesus mean when he said that the kingdom of heaven belongs to the little children?
—Why did the young man go away grieving?
—Why is salvation impossible for mortals but not for God?
—What did Jesus mean when he said that many who are first would be last, and the last would be first?

- Allow ample time for discussion.
- Reassemble the class and ask a representative from each group to report on the results of the group discussion. In the fourth act, point out that Jesus' answer is remarkable because he clearly states that there will be no reward except the reward of being with him. Just as disciples have received him on earth by receiving the little children, so will they be received as his brothers and sisters in heaven. In his presence all earthly distinctions are removed, for "many who are first will be last, and the last will be first."
- Record the reports on newsprint or chalkboard so that they may be reviewed and/or revised in light of the development of the rest of the lesson.

Dimension 2: What Does the Bible Mean?

Apparently many at Antioch considered their affluence as a sign of God's special favor and ignored the fact that the blessing of many possessions always carries with it the special obligation to provide for the needs of the poor. The problem of the affluent at Antioch was not that they *had* wealth but that they *valued* wealth more than the kingdom of heaven. The allegiance of their heart was misplaced. The misuse of their wealth resulted in their excluding themselves from the kingdom of heaven. They gained the whole world but forfeited their lives (16:24-26).

On the basis of a reading of 19:13-15, the most important decision for would-be disciples was the decision about how to treat the little children. It revealed what was valued most highly by the members of the community. Those who thought that they had already become disciples of Jesus by saying the right words about him had a problem. This text, however, confronted the would-be disciples in the church at Antioch with the fact that they could affirm Jesus as the Messiah, the Son of the living God, and at the same time refuse to follow him. The failure of would-be disciples was not the failure of words but the failure of action, the failure to receive the little children.

Matthew sought to correct this failure by helping the would-be disciples to see that they could not be with Jesus in the kingdom of God without being with the little children. His most powerful resource for making this point was Jesus' relationship with the children.

Jesus not only received the children but he also identified with them. He touched them, became as they were, powerless, unclean, sick, homeless, outcast, poor. He did this because of his obedience to God, whose will was that not one of the little ones should be lost (18:10-14).

Would-be disciples at Antioch could never become ideal disciples unless they perceived how Jesus was still present with them. He was with them not as the Messiah of Jewish nationalism, not as the Son of God of privilege and status, but as the Messiah of God's promise to be with the little children and as the Son of God who was gentle and humble in heart (1:18-25; 11:25-30). The Messiah was present with the church at Antioch in the little children (the poor, the sick, the lame, the blind, the outcast, and the powerless). The church of would-be disciples could never become ideal disciples unless they saw clearly that they needed to be with the little children because that was the only way they could be with Jesus and follow him into the kingdom of heaven.

(C) Experience community.

- Ask three class members to roleplay a situation. Without using costumes, one member should portray a poorly dressed person. As the person enters the room, she obviously feels out of place.
- Ask two other members to act as if they are repulsed by the stranger in their midst. They distance themselves from the needy person, ignoring this person. At this point in the drama the needy person holds up a placard with the name "JESUS" printed on it.
- The two other actors seem surprised at the revelation of the presence of Jesus in the needy person. Immediately they begin to reach out to the needy person. They are no longer withdrawn but embrace the one whom they have just excluded.
- Lead the class in a discussion of this drama by raising the following questions:
—Why is it that often we do not see that Jesus is present with us in needy persons (the little children)?
—If we exclude needy persons from our community for any reason, can we still claim that we are a Christian community?
—How do needy persons in our midst reveal to us our own real needs?
—Is the promise of the name *Emmanuel*, "God is with us," fulfilled for us when we recognize that Jesus is with us in the little children?
—Are we saved from our sins by the "little children"?
- Share the following information:
—Matthew used the dialogue between Jesus and the rich young man in 19:16-22 to help the church at Antioch identify what kept would-be disciples from becoming ideal disciples.
—The rich young man was determined to keep control of his life as an affluent and powerful member of society. Instead of reading Scripture to learn God's will and to submit to God's purpose for his life, he read Scripture to justify himself and to confirm his own special privilege. Jesus set before him an interpretation of Scripture that began with the nature of God. It insisted that a special relationship to God, who was perfect in love, carried with it a special responsibility to become perfect in love.

Jesus' words, "If you wish to be perfect," picked up the theme of inclusive love that he had developed in the Sermon on the Mount (5:43-48). The hindrance for would-be disciples in becoming ideal disciples was that they wanted their own will for their lives more than they wanted God's will.
—What did Jesus mean when he told the rich young man that to be perfect (to have treasure in heaven), he must go, sell his possessions, and give the money to the poor; then he should come and follow him? Clearly from the context Jesus told him to give up control over his own life, to stop trying to save himself, to let go of the security of the world, and to accept Jesus' way as the will of God for his life. In other words, Jesus told him exactly what he told every would-be disciple: "Truly I tell you, unless you change and become like children, you will never enter the kingdom of heaven." Since the young man wanted to stay the way he was more than he wanted to become a little child in the family of God, "he went away grieving."
—The text also made clear the fact that Jesus did not tell the young man that there was something that he could do that would reward him with eternal life or entrance into the Kingdom. Instead of telling him what he could *do*, Jesus told him what he must *become*. What he must become—a little child—was a human impossibilty. He could not transform himself into what God wanted him to be. That was a human impossibility as the disciples immediately perceived. But it was not a divine impossibility, because with God "all things are possible." God gave humans a new possibility by loving them perfectly in Jesus. It was only the experience of that love that could make would-be disciples want to leave everything, to become like little children, to follow Jesus, to have treasure in heaven.

(D) Experience an imaginary story.

The power of this text is dependent upon our own experiences of the transforming love of God in Jesus.
- Help the class to get in touch with its own experiences relating to the power of this text to change lives. Members may be hesitant to talk directly about a personal experience. However they may feel freer to discuss one indirectly if you lead them into an imaginary scene.
- Ask the class to join you in imagining a situation that unfolds around a mature, self-assured man who has risen to the top of his profession. He is respected and admired by his family, his colleagues, and his friends. He has encouraged other people to depend upon him and has been trustworthy in all his relationships. Now he has begun to entertain doubts about his achievements and about how other people evaluate his life. He gradually recognizes a contradiction between the way he really is and the way he would like to be seen. On the

surface all is well, but in his heart he carries a burden of anxiety and sorrow. Finally, he feels such alienation that he shuts other people out of his life. He becomes depressed to the point that he can no longer function normally. He checks himself into the psychiatric ward of a hospital. There he begins to change his view of himself. He recognizes his strengths and weaknesses, becomes receptive to the love and concern offered by his doctors, nurses, family, and friends. Later he describes his recovery as a process of becoming like a little child and gives the credit to the self-giving love of God revealed in the compassion of others.

- Guide reflection on this imaginary story by posing the following questions:
—Does a changed way of seeing ourselves often involve leaving what is false to follow what is true?
—Are we often challenged in the crisis of our lives to shift our trust from ourselves to another center of power?
—Is it possible for us to put our trust in the self-giving love of God without experiencing it in the words and deeds of others?
—Is there any connection between the way we understand God revealed in Jesus and the way we understand ourselves?

Matthew was aware of the fact that people expected to be rewarded for their actions. He did not argue with that expectation but rather led people to redefine what they meant by reward. The reward for becoming an ideal disciple was not to be confused with an earthly reward. An earthly reward was one given on the basis of merit and often created differences among people. On the contrary, the reward for becoming an ideal disciple was to live in dependence upon the love of God, to live in a community defined by that love, and to enjoy that love without consideration of merit or differences. The reward of ideal disciples was so incomparably greater than any earthly reward that when people saw it clearly they would want it enough to leave everything and follow Jesus for it.

The full force of Jesus' teaching about the reward of ideal disciples was a declaration that it was the only thing worth living for because it was the only thing that endured forever. Those who chose to be with Jesus in obedience to God would be rewarded in the Last Days by continuing to be with him. The quality of their relationship would be revealed by becoming brothers and sisters in the family of God. Eternal life was not measured by length of days lived but by breadth of compassion. Ideal disciples were those who left the exclusive and self-protective family of human society in order to enter the inclusive and self-giving family of the kingdom of heaven. Eternal life was being with God and with God's people by participating in the love of God revealed in Jesus. Jesus' statement, "But many who are first will be last, and the last will be first" (19:30), did not mean that the characterizing distinctions of human society would be perpetuated in the kingdom of heaven.

Jesus meant that in the kingdom of heaven the categories "first" and "last" would be meaningless because everyone would be "little ones" treasured by God.

(E) Rewrite a saying of Jesus.

- Distribute paper and pencils.
- Rewrite the saying of Jesus, "But many who are first will be last, and the last will be first," using none of the original wording.

Dimension 3: What Does the Bible Mean to Us?

The words of Jesus to the young man are immediately relevant for us, "If you wish to be perfect, go, sell your possessions, and give the money to the poor, and you will have treasure in heaven; then come, follow me." If we do not hear these words and obey them, then we will follow the young man instead of Jesus. We will go away from Jesus and his community into the sorrow of isolation and self-reliance.

The text teaches us that we need the little children in our lives because without them we cannot enter the kingdom of heaven.

Why, then, do we exclude the little children from our lives? Perhaps the answer lies in the fact that we think we need to protect ourselves from the little children more than we need to include them in our lives.

The little children confront us with the fact that only those who are saved from self-reliance will enter the kingdom of heaven.

The encounter between Jesus and the young man sets before us the radical difference between what we are taught by our society and what Jesus teaches us. Our society teaches us to seek to become aggressive, competitive, and independent. Jesus teaches us to become compassionate, cooperative, and interdependent. Our true strength comes not from excluding others and affirming ourselves but from including others and denying ourselves. The model for all would-be disciples is not the chief executive officers of corporate America but the perfection of God's love revealed in the words and deeds of Jesus.

No matter what our age or station in life, all of us who want to become disciples of Jesus must become little children.

This means that each time we experience Jesus' presence with us in the little children we are called to repentance. Repentance means leaving what we have become through our self-reliance to become what we can be through the grace of God in Jesus. This radical reorientation of our lives, this new beginning, this new birth, this new creation is a human impossibility. It is a gospel possibility because God's love revealed in Jesus is always with us in the little children. They come to us as God's reminder that what we *must* become we *can* become, because we have been included as little children in the kingdom of heaven.

Jesus' response to Peter's question about the reward of ideal disciples who have left everything to follow Jesus was intended to make us (would-be disciples) want to become ideal disciples.

The dramatic and vivid language about being with the glorified Son of man "at the renewal of all things" reminds us that eternal life is a quality of life that we have now when we choose to be members of the family of God. If we really *want* to have the quality of life that endures, then we will deny ourselves, take up our cross, and follow Jesus. The reward of ideal disciples is that they live in the household of God, the master of the house, as brothers and sisters of Jesus. The assumption of the text is that when would-be disciples see the ultimate importance of receiving the little children, then these would-be disciples will *want* with all their heart to receive the little children.

We must be careful not to misinterpret Jesus' teaching about the reward of receiving the little children. He did not say that the little children could be used to get something more important. *He said that the little children were the ultimate reward.* To receive them is to receive Jesus and God who sent Jesus (10:40-42). Therefore the reward of ideal disciples (eternal life, entrance into the kingdom of God) is to be with the little ones by becoming one of the little ones in the family of God. It is in this context that the hard saying at 10:37-39 must be understood: "Whoever loves father or mother more than me is not worthy of me; and whoever loves son or daughter more than me is not worthy of me; and whoever does not take up the cross and follow me is not worthy of me. Those who find their life will lose it, and those who lose their life for my sake will find it."

(F) Demonstrate the difference between Jesus and society.

- Create two scenes to bring out the contrast between the teaching of Jesus and the teaching of society.
- In the first scene a little child is playing in the living room of her home. She accidentally knocks a vase from the table and it shatters into pieces. An irate adult comes into the room, surveys the damage, and says impatiently to the child, "Why don't you grow up?"

- In the second scene an adult in a supervisory role is speaking sharply to an employee. The executive gives the employee a harsh reprimand, warns the employee that such incompetence will not be tolerated, then goes into an office and sits behind an impressive desk. Jesus is standing to one side observing the scene. Jesus comes into the office, glances around, looks intently at the executive, and then says sorrowfully to her or him, "Why did you grow up?"
- Conclude the exercise by asking the class the following questions:
—What is the difference between maturity in the eyes of the world and maturity in the eyes of Jesus?
—How does our society affirm us in our desire to be powerful and assertive?
—Is it possible to become what Jesus wants us to be and also to conform to society?

Additional Bible Helps

The parable of "the laborers in the vineyard" (20:1-16) develops the teaching of Jesus about the reward of disciples. The basis for the statement, "But many who are first will be last, and the last will be first," is the nature of the kingdom of heaven, "For the kingdom of heaven is like a landowner who went out early in the morning to hire laborers for his vineyard" (20:1). The action and dialogue of the parable leads to the conclusion, "So the last will be first, and the first last" (20:16). The power of the parable lies in the contrast between the expectations of the laborers about their wages (reward) and the behavior of the landowner. The laborers thought they would be paid different wages because of how long they had labored but the landowner paid them all the same wage because he was generous.

As Matthew understood this parable, connecting it with Jesus' blessing the little children and his encountering the rich young man, the surprise of the kingdom of heaven was that all who entered the Kingdom were little children who shared equally in the generosity of God. The kingdom of heaven does not preserve the distinctions "first" and "last" that are honored in human society but rather makes them meaningless. If we continue to expect rewards in the kingdom of heaven based on the assumption that we get what we earn, then we reveal that we still value earthly treasure more than heavenly treasure.

10
Matthew 21:1-17
THE MINISTRY OF JESUS THE MESSIAH AFFIRMED: THE PRAISE OF BABIES

LEARNING MENU
Again, remembering how your students learn best, choose to use at least one of the learning options provided for Dimensions 1, 2, and 3.

Dimension 1: What Does the Bible Say?

(A) Read the text dramatically.

For this session you will need class members to play these roles: NARRATOR, JESUS, the PROPHET, the CROWDS (represented by two or three persons), and the CHILDREN (represented by two or three persons).

(B) Answer the questions from the study book.

Turn to the questions in Dimension 1 that are listed on page 76 of the study book. Instruct class members to find a partner; each partner will share their answers with the other.
Possible answers include the following:
 1. Matthew speaks of two animals, presumably because of one interpretation of the prophecy found in verse 5.
 2. The crowds would have used the phrase "Son of David" to denote that Jesus was a royal figure, capable of ushering in an era of justice. *Hosanna* meant literally "O, save!" but often was used as a shout of praise.
 3. The bottom line is that God desired mercy rather than sacrifice.
 4. It would have been natural for Jesus to heal within the Temple, since the Temple was to engage in acts of mercy.
 5. Jesus challenged the authority of the religious leaders. The "least of these"—children, lame, blind, poor—were able to see clearly the divinity of Jesus. Those who were steeped in wisdom, such as the chief priests and scribes were blinded as to Jesus' identity.
 6. Yes!

(C) Examine Jesus' entry into Jerusalem.

Each episode in this story contains features with which the class is already familiar. The teacher must make a decision about how to deal with what the class already knows so as to help move the class to a richer understanding and a deeper commitment. The following observations about each episode are offered to stimulate you to develop the teaching strategies that will help you and the class to experience the creative power of the texts.

Jesus' entry into Jerusalem confronts the reader with the awareness that something unexpected took place:

—Jesus established his location at the Mount of Olives instead of in Jerusalem. The text tells us that Jesus was in opposition to Jerusalem because he understood messiahship quite differently from the way it was understood in Jerusalem.

—Jesus' choice of a donkey and a colt to ride into the city was another departure from the expected. Apparently Matthew misunderstood the poetic parallelism in Zechariah 9:9 as a reference to two different animals instead of one. Since the text seemed to require *two* animals, Matthew had Jesus fulfill the Scriptures by riding on two animals. However, the more surprising aspect of Jesus' entry was not the number of beasts on which he rode but the *kind* of beast he rode. In the ancient world a donkey was not the kind of animal a king rode. Jesus was definitely not the Davidic king of popular expectation.

—Jesus' entry threw the whole city into turmoil. When the crowds accompanying Jesus were asked about his identity, they answered in a way that revealed how little they knew about him, "This is the prophet Jesus from Nazareth in Galilee." So the story presented Jesus as the king but he is the king whom nobody knows.

—Another unexpected part of this story was what happened when Jesus entered the Temple and drove out the merchants and money changers. Those who were selling and buying in the Temple were providing the essentials for carrying out the religious activities of the Temple, paying tithes (taxes), and offering sacrifices. What had gone wrong in the Temple was not the introduction of secular activities into the sacred sphere, but the misunderstanding of the kind of activity that God required.

—The story contrasts the anger of the chief priests and the scribes in the Temple with the praise of the children. The chief priests and the scribes represent the arrogant and hard of heart who carry the heavy burden of self-righteousness. The children represent the gentle and humble in heart who find rest for their souls. If the children represent the blind and the lame who came to Jesus in the Temple and were cured, then the text affirms that only those who need mercy and receive it are able to give God acceptable praise. What kept the chief priests and the scribes from joining the children's chorus of praise in the Temple? They could not praise God because they were blinded by their hardness of heart and paralyzed by their sense of privilege. Their problem was not that they were blind but that they were blind and claimed to see perfectly. Similarly, their problem was not that they were lame but that they were lame and claimed to be without blemish. Is there any hope for the chief priests and the scribes? The answer is no, at least not from the viewpoint of human possibility. But the answer is yes from the viewpoint of divine possibility. "For God all things are possible" (19:26).

(D) Explore the meaning of *hosanna*.

One of the key words in the lesson is *hosanna*. It is a transliteration of a Hebrew expression that literally means "Save now, we pray." Used in this context, *hosanna* is an exclamation of adoration, praise, and great joy.

- Assign the class the task of identifying contemporary words that we use to express similar feelings.
- List words identified by class members on chalkboard or newsprint.
- Reflect on the difference between understanding biblical words *intellectually* and understanding them *experientially*.
- Invite the class to stand and shout the word *hosanna*.
- Invite class members to discuss with a partner the meaning of the word *hosanna*.
- Record these interpretations on newsprint or chalkboard.
- Ask class members to shout *hosanna* again.
- Invite class members to share with each other the feelings that are aroused by the sound of the word.
- Close this exercise by asking the class to try to remember some experience of adoration, praise, and joy that helps them to become like little children crying out in the Temple, "Hosanna to the Son of David!"

Dimension 2: What Does the Bible Mean?

(E) Imagine Jesus' entry.

Ancient Jerusalem was not a city of peace. The average citizen was oppressed by a heavy burden of taxation imposed by Rome, by the local political authorities who served Rome's purposes, and by the Temple bureaucracy. It was torn by racial and religious hatreds. It was afflicted by the disease and pestilence bred by a foul water supply, no sewage disposal, and crowded living quarters. It was haunted by the memory of past glory and frustrated by hopes of a better future that were never realized. It was a city in which peace was an empty dream.

- Provide the class with modeling clay, crayons and paper, and pencils and paper.
- Instruct class members to use the medium with which they are most comfortable to create images of the welcome received by Jesus when he entered Jerusalem as the King of Peace. Provide time for sharing the images and then focus the discussion by raising the following issues:

—In what sense was Jesus the King of Peace?

—Why did his coming into Jerusalem throw the city into turmoil and provoke the anger of the chief priests and the scribes?

—Who was responsible for the conditions in Jerusalem that kept the city from becoming a place of peace?

This lesson is often used to justify angry and impulsive reactions to evil. The text does not support such an interpretation. Jesus did not act in a fit of anger. He acted out of his obedience to God's will as revealed to him in Scripture. The emphasis in the text falls upon Jesus' submission to his vocation. His authority consisted in his dependence upon God and his desire to please God more than the political and religious authorities of Jerusalem. He was able to drive the representatives of evil from the Temple because of his unwavering trust in the goodness of God.

The word *cleanse* is not found in the text but this word has been imposed upon the text and used to interpret it. What Jesus said and did in the Temple did not cleanse it, however.

The action develops around a confrontation in the Temple between those who were doing the wrong thing in the Temple and Jesus, who wanted to do the right thing in the Temple. The Temple bureaucracy (represented by the money changers, merchants, chief priests, and scribes) did not do the right thing in the Temple because they did not know what God wanted. Jesus, however, did the right thing in the Temple because he knew what God wanted in God's house. Jesus' words and deeds in the Temple did not *cleanse* the Temple but rather they *judged* the Temple authorities because they had claimed the Temple as their own and made it into a den of robbers.

The standard of judgment for everything done in the Temple was the mercy of God. One of the startling conclusions that the text supports is that only those actions which express the mercy of God are acceptable in the Temple. It seems that Jesus aroused anger and opposition among the Temple authorities by insisting in his words and his deeds that the most correct tithes and sacrifices in the Temple were completely unacceptable to God unless they included those who needed and sought God's mercy. Jesus pronounced judgment upon the Temple authorities not because they failed to perform their rituals correctly but because they failed to practice mercy. Their actions were fundamentally wrong because they thought that they could hallow God's name in the Temple without including the blind and the lame and offering them God's compassion.

Jesus was the servant of God because his special relationship to God was expressed in his special responsibility for God's little ones. He came, "not to be served but to serve, and to give his life a ransom for many" (20:28). The Temple in Jerusalem was a symbol of the special relationship between God and God's people. But that special relationship had been violated and misinterpreted by those who should have known better. They had rejected their special responsibility to serve others because they were preoccupied with their special privileges. Thus they sought to draw near to God by excluding others and by misusing Scripture to protect themselves. The result was that the more rigorously they practiced their religion the more they separated themselves from God and God's little ones. Jesus was an offense to them. As the servant of God he showed them what God wanted them to become and what God required them to do.

(F) Read dramatically.

- Choose members of the class to play the following roles:
  the NARRATOR, MOTHER OF THE SONS OF ZEBEDEE (JAMES AND JOHN), JAMES, JOHN, JESUS, AND THE TEN OTHER DISCIPLES.
- Read Matthew 20:20-28, dramatizing it as you have in earlier class sessions.
- After the narrative has been presented, lead the class in a discussion of the following questions:

—Why did the mother of James and John approach Jesus and kneel before him?
—What was the significance of Jesus' asking her, "What do you want?"
—To what does "drink the cup" refer?
—Why were the ten other disciples angry with the two brothers?
—What did Jesus tell the disciples about the difference between his kingship and the kingship of the Gentiles?
—Can you identify connecting links between the conflict in this narrative and the conflict in the Temple?

The contrast between the chief priests, scribes, and Jesus arose from the priorities of their lives. The priority for the chief priests and the scribes was to protect themselves and their institution from being defiled by the presence of the blind and the lame, the unclean. The priority for Jesus was to identify with the blind and the lame and to cure them by giving himself for them. Jesus sought to reform the Temple not by excluding God's little ones but by including them and offering them the mercy that they needed. They greeted him as their King because he was with them as a little child. He treated them with the dignity and respect of the children of God.

The blind and the lame were an offense to the chief priests and the scribes because they interfered with the religious activities of the Temple. Since the collection of the Temple tax and the offering of sacrifices were the right way to honor God, the needs of the little ones were distractions that had to be overcome in order to please God. Jesus redefined the action that was pleasing to God by affirming in his words and deeds that the Temple was made holy by welcoming the little ones. He made room for them at the center of his life. Doing so was the way he declared his allegiance to God and submitted himself to the will of God. The little ones were not a distraction to him but the revelation of God's power and presence that taught him the meaning of the Scriptures: "I desire steadfast love and not sacrifice" (Hosea 6:6).

Jesus was received by the little ones with a cry of adoration, delight, and praise because he gave himself for them. Their praise was not the calculated and self-conscious response of those who wanted to promote their own status and power. It was the spontaneous overflow of those who wanted to give themselves completely to a power greater than themselves. They knew him as their King because he had revealed himself to them as the King of Peace who was "gentle and humble in heart."

(G) Stage an interruption.

- In advance of the session, plan for a disruption of the class by the sudden appearance of little children.
- Arrange for the teachers of small children in the Sunday school to interrupt the class by bringing the children into the class.
- Encourage the children to play a game during the adult session, as you attempt to continue with teaching the class.
- Finally respond to the children in ways that affirm their presence and acknowledge their importance.
- When the children have departed, raise the following questions:
—Do our actions ever contradict our statements about the importance of little children?
—How do the little children minister to us?
—How do the little children make us aware of our responsibility for the powerless of all ages?
—Is it possible for us to welcome God and Christ into our lives without welcoming the little children?

Dimension 3: What Does the Bible Mean to Us?

- Share the following information with class members. This lesson helps us to see three different responses to Jesus' ministry.
—The *first response* is to be found in the crowds who accompanied Jesus into Jerusalem.
—The *second response* is represented by the chief priests and scribes who became angry when Jesus cured the blind and the lame in the Temple.
—The *third response* is represented by the blind and the lame who were cured by Jesus and who offered him the authentic praise of little children: "Hosanna to the Son of David!"

The intent is to help the reader avoid the example of the crowds, the chief priests and the scribes, and to follow the example of the little children. One of the persistent problems of would-be disciples is the difference between what we want Jesus to be and what Jesus really is. If we follow Jesus because we think he will give us what we want, then inevitably we are going to be disappointed. Why? Because Jesus does not conform to what we *want* but what we *need*. We do not need to follow a king who will give us an advantage over our foes, who will sanction our violent and cruel impulses, who will affirm our greed and selfishness. Rather we need to follow a king who reconciles us with our foes, who condemns our violent and cruel impulses, who encourages our generosity and compassion. The king who conforms to our wants has no power to save us from our sins. But Jesus, the King of Peace, saves us from our sins because he has the power to make us want what we need.

Jesus does this for us not through coercion or manipulation but by the giving of himself for us. We then are moved by his love to want to be like him.

One fundamental standard of judgment must be applied to all that we do in the service of God—mercy. When we make our decisions about ritual, we must make sure they are merciful. When we design our polity, we must invoke the standard of mercy. When we weigh our moral options, we must temper them with mercy. None of this can ever be done in abstract but always in the context of the little ones, the least, the last, and the lost at the margins of our society. Their cries must be heard in our churches and all the resources of our churches must be available to them. Why? Because the church is built upon the revelation of God in Jesus. He is the one who puts the children in our midst, who takes them in his arms, and warns us that if we attempt to enter the kingdom of God without becoming like them all our efforts will be fruitless.

Perhaps the word *king* is so firmly associated in our minds with images of power, coercion, violence, tyranny, and self-indulgence that it can no longer function for us in the way it was intended. We may be closer to the truth revealed in Jesus when we welcome him into our lives as God's special child. In his gentleness and humility he shows us how we all appear in the sight of God. We see in him what God wants us to be. We experience in him the mercy that cures us of our blindness and lameness so that we join the children's chorus in the praise that God has prepared for himself.

(H) Welcome the child.

- Reflect on the idea of Jesus coming into our lives as God's special child. Prepare the scene by telling the class to imagine they are part of a crowd sitting on the lawn of a public building. Word has spread that a great person is about to make a triumphant entry into the city. The crowd is waiting expectantly. No police escort, no stretch limousine, no military band has yet appeared when someone shouts, "There he [or she] is!" The great one comes into view. There is a gasp from the crowd. The great one is a *little child* who comes into the city pedaling a tricycle.

- Reflect on the scene by raising the following questions:
—How does this scene shed light on the Scripture?
—How does the Scripture help to interpret this scene?
—Are we so controlled by our adult inhibitions and preconceptions that we are often unable to use our imaginations creatively?

(I) Develop a litany of thanksgiving.

- Ask class members to develop a litany in which members share those things for which they are thankful that the world would consider inconsequential. In Jesus' day these things were represented by the lame, the blind, and the children. What might they be today? AIDS victims? Children? Mentally or physically challenged individuals?
- In developing the litany, use the phrase, "Thank you, God, for teaching us eternal truths through _____

Additional Bible Helps

Matthew used these texts about Jesus' entrance into Jerusalem and his judgment of the Temple to help the church at Antioch understand that Jesus' kingship was radically different from the kingships of the world. Jesus did not conform to popular expectations about how he would act because his allegiance was centered in God instead of in the crowds. As God's Messiah, his role was to do God's will, to deny himself, to serve others, and to find his life by losing it. Just as Jesus did not belong to Jerusalem and did not accept the religious activities of the Temple, so he did not belong to the church at Antioch and did not accept the religious activities of the church.

The church authorities in Antioch were no different from the chief priests and the scribes in Jerusalem. When they used Scripture to exclude the blind and the lame and to protect themselves, they were robbers who, in the guise of honoring God, denied God. Matthew responded to the crisis in the church at Antioch by focusing attention upon the traditions about what Jesus had said and done in Jerusalem. He was confident that his witness about how Jesus was present in the past would make the church sensitive to his presence now. Since he was present as God's Messiah in the church at Antioch, the would-be disciples could become ideal disciples. They could leave everything, become little children, and offer acceptable praise to God.

Jesus defined what royalty meant. For him royalty did not mean the arrogance of privilege and the cruelty of self-indulgence but the gentleness of service and the compassion of self-giving. His royal presence was not acknowledged by those who sought to make him behave like all the kings of the world but by those who greeted him as their King because he had renounced all the privileges of kingship. He was the promised Messiah in a way that contradicted all the narrow and exclusive ambitions of nationalism. His authentic disciples were those who had been blessed by his presence and who wanted to be like him in dependence upon God and in service to others.

His royal presence did not divide people into hostile camps. He came as the agent of God's promised salvation to all the nations of the earth. He was not simply against war; he was for peace. Those who looked for a warrior king riding triumphantly on a war horse at the head of a conquering army would never recognize the King of Peace riding humbly on a donkey in the midst of confused and bewildered crowds.

Jesus was always the victorious King of Peace because in the power of his self-giving love all the powers of evil had been overcome. In him God's inclusive community was established and it awaited all who sought to enter it. Peace was the establishment of God's will on earth as in heaven. That meant the end of injustice, of hatred, of greed, of self-righteousness. The tension in the text was not accidental or temporary. It was created by what Jesus had to do because of his vocation and was always present because of the resistance he encountered not only among his opponents but also among his followers. Everything hung in the balance in Antioch. It did so not because Jesus' future was dependent upon how he was received in Antioch but because Antioch's future was dependent upon how he was received in Antioch. The peace of the city as well as the peace of the church was riding with the King of Peace; but only those who wanted peace more than anything else would receive it.

11

Matthew 25:31-46

The Ministry of Jesus the Messiah Now and Not Yet: The Coming Judgment

LEARNING MENU

Perhaps the greatest challenge you will face as you lead this lesson is that the concept of a Final Judgment has been trivialized or reduced to popular images. One of the most common of such images is that of the bearded prophet, dressed in a white robe, standing at a crowded intersection, proclaiming to an indifferent crowd, "Prepare to meet your God!"

Many people either ignore the Final Judgment completely or dismiss it as an irrelevant superstition. This subject requires careful consideration in order for people to take seriously one of the central emphases in the teaching of Jesus and one of the major concerns of Christian faith.

Keeping in mind the ways in which your class members learn best as well as their needs and interests, choose at least one learning segment from each of the three Dimensions.

Dimension 1: What Does the Bible Say?

It is clear from the picture of the Last Judgment in Matthew 25:31-46 that the event is a future expectation. It is "not yet." This future reference is also a central emphasis in the parables that lead up to the teaching about the judgment of the nations when the Son of man comes in his glory.

The parable of the faithful or the unfaithful slave (24:45-51) sets up a situation in which the master has gone away but is expected to return in the future. He is *not yet* present. The parable of the ten bridesmaids (25:1-13) also assumes a time when the bridegroom is expected but has *not yet* come. Likewise, there is a lapse of time in the parable of the talents (25:14-30) between the charge given to the slaves by their master and the day of reckoning when he returns. Without this future reference to a coming day of reckoning that is *not yet*, there is no urgency about the present and no ultimate seriousness about what is done *now*. So the importance of the *not yet* of Final Judgment is not *when* it will take place but *that it will* occur. All efforts to determine the hour or the day are futile and irrelevant. Such efforts shift attention from what one should be doing *now* to that which one has no control over and for which one has no responsibility (24:36-44).

How then should one prepare for the surprise of the *not yet*, the coming of the Son of man in glory to judge the nations? The three parables mentioned above as well as the parables of the wicked tenants (21:33-45) and the wedding banquet (22:1-14) teach that preparation for the coming Judgment is to live *now* as if the Judge were already present.

But what kind of activity is the right preparation for the unexpected hour of the coming of the Son of man? The answer, given in detail and with dramatic emphasis in 25:31-46, is that the only preparation for the Judgment of the Son of man in the *not yet* is to practice mercy *now*. What will occur at the Last Judgment will be the surprising revelation of how each one has ministered to the needs of the least of these *now*.

(A) Read the text dramatically.

- Follow the procedure used in each previous session to involve the class in the dramatic action of the text.
- Choose class members to portray the **narrator, king (Son of man), sheep, goats, angels,** and **people of the nations.**

(B) Create artistic images.

- Instruct the class to imagine the relevance of this text for their own lives by creating artistic images. Provide drawing paper, modeling clay, or other art supplies.
- Ask class members to create an image that expresses how they feel about the dramatic Scripture reading.
- After showing their creations to the whole group, ask:
—Were there common feelings among the group? unique feelings?
—What feelings were expressed about each of the characters in the reading?

(C) Answer the study book questions.

Possible answers to the questions on page 84 in the study book include the following:

1. God's glory is God's manifestation in the world. The glory of the Son of man reflects his importance to God and to the world, especially as it reveals God.

2. The passage refers to both "this worldly" and "next worldly" depictions as they converge at an End time; the totality of all that is. "All nations" includes not just the neat world view of "my community" but of all communities of God's creation.

3. Both "sheep" and "goats" will be surprised by what their action or inaction has accomplished without their knowing it. Deeds done of love without thought for reward will reap everlasting reward. Deeds left undone will result in an eternal torment to those who were thoughtless toward Christ and "the least."

4. The "least" are those who are most vulnerable in their society: the ill, the poor, and so on. But Jesus exists among them as a constant and hidden presence.

Dimension 2: What Does the Bible Mean?

(D) Provide information on the Final Judgment.

Introduce material from "The Final Judgment" in Additional Bible Helps to your class members. If you choose to present this information in lecture format, do so briefly. Class members could present this information; provide them with the information printed below and encourage them to do further research in your church library or public library.

(E) Simulate a service of Holy Communion.

- As a group, simulate a service of Holy Communion. One class member acts as the celebrant, the others as communicants. Identify one communicant as a goat and all other communicants as sheep. All communicants come forward to be served. Ask the celebrant to confront the goat and send him or her away.
- Now simulate another service of Holy Communion. Again have one person act as the celebrant, the others as communicants. Identify all the communicants as well as the celebrant as goats. Ask the celebrant to welcome everyone to be served.
- Lead the class in a discussion of the issues raised by the simulations.
- Offer the following questions to stimulate participation:
—How does exclusion hinder the practice of mercy?
—How does inclusion promote the practice of mercy?
—Is it possible for people to practice mercy if they have not received mercy?
—What examples of inclusion and exclusion are you able to identify in the world? in the church?

Dimension 3: What Does the Bible Mean to Us?

(F) Identify how we prepare for major life events.

Each of us has prepared for major events in our lives and in the lives of others—weddings, births, graduations, ordinations, confirmations, employment, retirement, even death—sometimes several of these events in one season!

- Invite class members to brainstorm the steps involved with "getting ready" for major events in our lives.

- Note the offerings of class members on newsprint or chalkboard.

(G) Identify how Christians prepare for the Second Coming.

- In small groups of three, consider the following questions:
—Since we do not know when the Son of man will return, what must we do to prepare?
—Since we do not know when the Son of man will return, what must we not do as we wait?
—How do you feel about the Second Coming?
- Lead a group discussion bringing out the following information in the class:

The early Christians had a problem with the Final Judgment. They were so preoccupied with the *when* of his Second Coming that they neglected to get ready for it. Modern Christians, on the other hand, have become so forgetful of the fact that he is coming that they have neglected to get ready.

The results of mistaken emphases about the Final Judgment were the same then as now. People failed to use their time and their resources responsibly to get ready for a day of accountability.

Matthew's solution to this problem was to remind disciples that the Son of man was always present among the needy. This is where we must begin to recover a sense of urgency about our daily lives and the only way that we can begin to get ready *now* for the *not yet* of his coming in glory. If we do not believe that he has already come as the gentle and humble Son of man, nothing will ever convince us that he is coming as the glorified and triumphant Son of man.

Speculation about Jesus' return, regardless of the form it takes, is a distraction that keeps us from doing what we ought to do. He has told us what we ought to do in one word: have *mercy*.

(H) Experience faith.

- Select two persons from the class to demonstrate the difference between accepting facts about a person and putting one's trust in a person.
- Prepare two scenes. In the first scene: person A greets person B. A tells B certain facts, such as age, weight, height, occupation, and so forth. B responds by saying, "I believe you."

In the second scene, A tells B, "I know you are trustworthy and I have confidence in you." B responds by saying, "You are a friend and our relationship is precious to me." They embrace warmly.

One of the major emphases of the text is that the surprise of Final Judgment will lie in the discovery of what is really important. Things that seem to be of paramount importance will be disclosed as worthless. Things that seem to be worthless will be disclosed as having paramount importance. Appearances are in fact misleading. People in high places who possess wealth and have authority over others seem to be worthy of our attention and our honor. People in need who have no wealth and are powerless seem to be unworthy of our attention and our honor. Often we are so deceived by appearances that we refuse to pay attention to those who are really in need. Our lives are impoverished as a result.

(I) Question our values.

- Clip pictures from current magazines that portray people from a wide range of social, economic, and cultural backgrounds. Be sure to include pictures of people who are obviously affluent and people who are obviously needy.
- Display the pictures on a table so that the class will have easy access to them.
- Instruct the class to select pictures of people with whom they would want to be associated. Caution members not to choose according to how they think they *ought* to behave but according to how they *do* behave. Each member of the class should make a number of choices.
- Ask members of the class to identify the people whom they have chosen and to tell why they made their choices.
- Reflect on the experience by raising several questions. If your class is large, invite persons to form groups of three. Assign one question to each small group.
—Should we ever give or withhold mercy on the basis of appearances?
—Can we ever know who are the truly needy?
—Can you think of an instance when Jesus refused to give mercy to those who asked for it?
—Why is the discovery that mercy is all that really matters such a surprise?
- Invite each small group to report highlights from their small group discussion so that the entire class has the benefit of several different viewpoints.

God does not change. God's mercy is from everlasting to everlasting. How we respond to God's mercy determines whether we are *blessed by mercy received* or *damned by mercy rejected*. We receive hope from the text because it reminds us that the kingdom of heaven is at hand in the life and ministry of Jesus. Since the Kingdom is always here in the least of these, we can receive it with joy now and forever. "Truly I tell you, unless you change and become like children, you will never enter the kingdom of heaven. Whoever becomes humble like this child is the greatest in the kingdom of heaven. Whoever welcomes one such child in my name welcomes me" (18:3-5).

(J) Create a contemporary parable.

The imagery of the Final Judgment in the Bible is often so strange to modern Christians that it is virtually incomprehensible.

- Lead the class in an effort to change the imagery so that the lessons will be more applicable.
- Develop a contemporary parable along these lines:

A husband and wife have lived together for years and have become comfortable with their routine. The wife's parents are elderly and afflicted with serious illnesses. She is the only caregiver for them in their closing years. Periodically she is called away from home to care for her parents. When she leaves her husband, he always asks, "When are you coming back?" Her reply is always the same, "I don't know when, but I'll be back."

After his wife has gone, the husband neglects the routine of housekeeping for a few days. Then he begins to follow her housekeeping routines in her absence. He finds himself doing the chores the way she would have done them. Before long he finds himself living in her absence exactly the way he lives in her presence. One day he receives word that his wife is coming home. It is a joyful occasion. He greets her at the airport, and they drive to their home together. She finds it clean and in order. The reason the husband had their home in good order was not because he knew when to prepare for her arrival. The reason was because he knew what she wanted done and how she wanted it done.

- In small groups of three discuss:
—What does this modern parable tell us about "getting ready"?
—Consider the results and feelings of the husband and wife if he had forgotten her wishes during the time she was gone.

(K) Share viewpoints about the Second Coming.

The Second Coming is a difficult concept for many Christians; many avoid talking about it.

- Divide the class into groups of two. Instruct partners to spend some time discussing the Second Coming. Use the following questions as discussion starters.
—When you think about the Second Coming, what comes to your mind?
—Is this a critical issue for Christians today? Should it be?
—Do you think there is too much emphasis on this one theme in Christianity? Why, or why not?

(L) Sing.

- Provide hymnbooks for the class.
- Find hymns about the Second Coming.
- Using paper and pencil, make two columns on your paper.
- Place titles of hymns that best represent your thinking about the Second Coming in one column.
- Place titles of hymns that do not represent your thinking about the Second Coming in the other section.
- Discuss the following questions:
—What seems to be the predominant themes in hymns that focus on the Second Coming?
—During what historical period were these hymns composed?
- Randomly, invite individuals to identify one hymn from each column. Sing at least the first stanza of each.

Additional Bible Helps

The motifs of 25:31-46 are taken from the standard imagery of Jewish apocalyptic literature. The word *apocalyptic* is an adjective derived from the Greek word *apocalyptein*, which means "to reveal or disclose." Apocalyptic literature is literature that reveals or discloses mysteries or secrets about the end of time. The imagery of apocalyptic literature is poetic and metaphorical. It appeals to the emotions rather than to logic. It presents vivid pictures rather than reasoned arguments. This literature flourished in Jewish and Christian circles from about 200 B.C.E. to 200 C.E. Examples of Hebrew apocalyptic literature are found in Daniel 7—12; Isaiah 24—27 and 56—66; Ezekiel 37—48; Zechariah 9—14. The best known examples of Christian apocalyptic literature are Matthew 24; Mark 13; Luke 21; and Revelation.

The Final Judgment

A conviction that was widespread among the followers of Jesus was that he would come quickly to consummate the Kingdom and bring the world to an end. The fact that he did not come during the first generation of believers created a problem for some disciples. Matthew addressed this problem by reminding the church that Jesus taught that the time of his coming in glory could not be known (24:36-44); therefore the disciples needed to be continually in a state of preparation (24:45-51).

Jesus' coming was a matter of urgency for the church, not because it was soon to occur, but because it was certain to occur. The task of the church was not to speculate about when he would come. It was to get ready for his coming by hearing and doing his word. They were to live obediently *now* as if he were already present. Life was urgent and full of meaning because it offered the opportunity to prepare for the end by living each day as if it were the last.

Jesus' teaching about the Last Judgment by the Son of man did not add anything new to the teaching he had given his disciples from the beginning of his public ministry. Now as he drew near the end of his earthly ministry, he persisted in the central emphasis of his words and deeds. The most important lesson that his disciples needed to learn from him was to value divine things more than human things. He had not left them to puzzle about the meaning of divine things. He had defined the meaning in his ministry when he showed mercy on Matthew, a hated tax collector. He had welcomed him into the community of his followers. He drove home the point of his action by ordering his critics, the Pharisees, "Go and learn what this means, 'I desire mercy, not sacrifice.' For I have come to call not the righteous but sinners" (9:13). In this saying, the word *sacrifice* was a symbol for the practice of religion that excluded those who were in need: the children, the little ones, the least of these, the sick, the blind, the lame, the unclean, the despised, the rejected, the tax collectors, and the sinners. Jesus included all of them because God included them. He even included the Pharisees, the scribes, the elders, and the chief priests. But not even Jesus could make them receive the mercy that they did not want.

Jesus revealed to his disciples and to his foes the nature of God. Therefore, his action did not conform to what people wanted but to what God wanted. When a conflict arose between what God wanted and what the Temple authorities wanted, God prevailed. When there was a conflict between what God wanted and what the disciples wanted, God prevailed. When there was a conflict between what God wanted and what the crowd wanted, God prevailed. God prevailed wherever Jesus was because Jesus' will conformed to the will of God. Jesus always chose the course of action that was right. Those who opposed Jesus, for whatever reason, revealed that they opposed God because they did not know the meaning of this statement: "I desire mercy and not sacrifice."

The people who opposed Jesus because of his ministry of mercy were convinced that they were doing the right thing. The teaching of Jesus about the Last Judgment in 25:31-46 made it clear that strong conviction about how one had lived was not the basis for judgment. All that mattered in an ultimate sense was whether or not the hungry had been fed, the thirsty had been given drink, the stranger had been welcomed, the naked had been clothed, the sick had received care, and the prisoner had been visited. All of these actions were right because they were manifestations of mercy. What made an action wrong was its failure to express mercy.

The text taught that there was no way to avoid the surprise of the Final Judgment. The sheep would be as surprised as the goats. Therefore one should practice mercy in the present so that when the Son of man came in glory the surprise of the Final Judgment would be an eternal blessing instead of an eternal punishment.

An assumption that seems to be made in the text is that when people do what they really want to do they may be surprised by the consequences. The sheep, who practice mercy, lose themselves in acts of charity. They do not minister to the needs of others to obtain a blessing. But they are startled to discover that by losing themselves they find themselves.

The goats, who do not practice mercy, protect themselves by acts of selfishness. They refuse to minister to the needs of others in order to cling to their possessions, to protect themselves from them. They are startled to discover that by seeking to save themselves they have lost themselves.

Sheep and goats are used metaphorically in the text to represent the good people who have practiced mercy and the wicked people who have not practiced mercy. Until the Final Judgment, there is no difference in their appearance. Only the Son knows whether they are sheep or goats. At his coming, he will separate them. This stern warning is for all people: it is not their role to pronounce judgment upon others. To conclude that this text teaches people to classify others is a misuse of the text. Instead of the text promoting arrogance and self-righteousness, it encourages humility and self-examination. Judgment is reserved for the Son of man alone. The text intends to call the people of the nations to repent so that the Final Judgment will be a day of blessing rather than a day of punishment. People are not condemned by the text to eternal punishment. On the contrary, they are encouraged by it to begin to do those things *now* that will make them heirs of the Kingdom prepared for them from the foundation of the world.

Each person addressed by the text is potentially either a sheep or a goat. The text teaches that the choices one makes *now* determine what one will be in the *not yet* of the Final Judgment. The *not yet* of Final Judgment is *now*.

The Final Judgment is actually what we do to ourselves. If we have refused to give mercy to our brothers and sisters and have used our religion to exclude them from our lives, then we will discover that God gives us what we choose: eternal separation. If we have given mercy to our brothers and sisters and have used our religion to include them in our lives, then we will discover that God gives us what we choose: eternal community.

12 The Ministry of Jesus the Messiah Completed: Agony and Triumph

Matthew 26:30-46

LEARNING MENU
Keep in mind the ways in which your class members learn best as you choose one or more teaching methods from Dimensions 1, 2, and 3.

Dimension 1: What Does the Bible Say?

The contrast between Jesus and the disciples is a literary technique that Matthew used to help his readers experience the difference between confidence in self and confidence in God. It is not enough to be aware of using contrast as a literary technique. You must also strive to get class members to *experience* the contrast as two radically different ways of understanding the nature of authentic authority and real power. The text shows that those who seem to exercise authority and wield power are in fact powerless while the one who seems to be without authority or power is in fact powerful.

(A) Answer questions from the study book.

Reflect on the questions from Dimension 1 in the study book. Possible answers include the following:

1. Peter may have spoken aloud what others were thinking, but he appears in this passage to be overly confident of his own abilities (33) only to discover that he is as human as his colleagues (40).

2. Understandably, Jesus experiences human emotions as he faces leaving those he loves to face the cross.

3. The hour is late. The disciples are tired. This passage shows the human frailties of those called to follow Jesus.

4. Jesus prays for deliverance but also the ability to do God's will.

(B) Read the text dramatically.

- Use the skills that the class has already developed in reading the text dramatically. Select the following actors: a NARRATOR, JESUS, PETER, JAMES, JOHN, and EIGHT OTHER DISCIPLES.
- Set the stage so that two related scenes will unfold (1) the dialogue between Jesus, Peter, and the disciples on the Mount of Olives and (2) the agony and triumph of Jesus against the background of the sleeping disciples in Gethsemane.
- In the first scene the action focuses on the exchange between Jesus and Peter but the presence of the other disciples is included and essential to the dramatic development.

  The climax of the scene occurs when the ten disciples

surround Jesus and repeat as a chorus Peter's words of protest: "Even though I must die with you, I will not deny you" (26:35).
- In the second scene Jesus dominates the action and is without doubt the center of attention. He is the one who tells the eight disciples what to do and he commands Peter, James, and John to come with him and to keep awake with him. Set the stage so that Jesus' leaving and returning to them are obvious.
- Reflect on the experience. Invite each actor to report on his or her feelings about the drama.
- Conclude the exercise by asking each member of the class to imagine how he or she would have participated in the drama. This will help the class to engage the text at the level of their own faith journey. They may begin to see that no matter where we may be or what we may be doing, we are confronted with the choices that Jesus and his disciples made.
- Discuss the question, Will we follow the example of Jesus or the example of the disciples?

Dimension 2: What Does the Bible Mean?

The crucial issue that Jesus and his disciples faced on the Mount of Olives was the question of the object of their faith. The decision that they made would determine whether or not they would meet the test of Gethsemane. If they were triumphant in Gethsemane, then they would be victorious when they were delivered up to the chief priests and scribes, condemned to death, sentenced by Pilate, and executed on Golgotha.

Jesus and his disciples parted company because of the choices that they made in their hour of trial. Jesus entered the narrow gate and took the hard road that led to life. The disciples entered the wide gate and took the easy road that led to destruction. The events that unfolded confirmed the truth of what Jesus had taught them in the Sermon on the Mount (7:13-14).

(C) Provide background to the text.

Use the information in the Additional Bible Helps to help class members understand the background of the Scripture. This information may be provided in a mini-lecture format.

(D) Discuss faith as being a mind set on divine things.

- Begin the discussion by stating that the Greek word for mind is *nous*, which does not refer to our mental faculties but to the innermost core of our being. To set one's mind on divine things is to be turned toward God and God's will with all one's being. Our basic problem seems to be that we allow human things to occupy the center of our attention and to claim our highest allegiance.
- Lead a discussion of Jesus' dialogue with Peter in 26:30-35. Raise the following questions:
—How does Jesus reveal that his mind is set on divine things?
—How do Peter and the ten disciples reveal that their minds are set on human things?
—Identify divine things in your own experience.
—Identify the human things on which you have set your mind.
—Describe a situation in which you had to choose between divine and human things.
—Did your choice reveal the object of your faith?
- Share the following information:
—Although Jesus did not condemn his disciples for failing to stay awake with him in his hour of trial, it is clear that he expected them to enter into his agony and to triumph with him. Matthew used the traditions he had received about this event to help his readers see the awful consequences of misplaced faith and also to help them to place confidence in God. The text, then, was not so much a prediction of failure as it was a call to repentance. The text offers another possibility to all would-be followers of Jesus. However, that possibility was available only to those who recognized that trust in themselves, in their institutions, in their power, and in their own authority would lead them to destruction.
—The text seems to affirm that release from the bondage of self-confidence never comes easy. It is not a head trip but a heart trip involving the totality of one's being.
—Peter and the other disciples were asked to leave the human things in their lives that were obviously evil. They were also asked to leave the human things that were often honored and applauded because they seemed to be good.
—They were placed in a situation that seemed to require their independence, courage, and self-reliance. What seemed to be required was in fact inappropriate for those who wanted to be followers of one whose vocation was mercy and whose way was the path of gentle humble service.

(E) Reflect on Peter's denial of Jesus.

The portrayal of Peter's denial of Jesus in the courtyard of the high priest (26:57-75) is one of the most vivid characterizations in all of literature. Much of its power derives from the contrast with Jesus on trial before the council.
—Whereas Jesus, when questioned by the high priest three times, made no defense of himself, Peter, when accused

by servant girls and bystanders three times, vehemently defended himself.
—Jesus revealed how one saved one's life by losing it. Peter revealed how one lost one's life by saving it.
—Jesus was condemned to death while Peter seemed to go free.
- Lead the class in reflecting on the scene by considering the following questions:
—Why did Jesus remain silent?
—Why did Peter protest his innocence?
—Why did Peter follow Jesus at a distance?
—Does following Jesus at a distance always deprive one of the joy of being with Jesus? Does it always doom one to the sorrow of going out and weeping bitterly?
- If your class is large, divide the class into groups of three, and assign to each group one of the questions.
- If you discuss the questions in smaller groups, invite those groups to share highlights of the discussion with the entire class. Note on chalkboard or newsprint significant points.

The text is unequivocal in its proclamation that Jesus' confidence in God resulted in his passing through the agony of his hour of trial to the triumph of his resurrection.

The triumph of Jesus was not in any sense a victory that he achieved on his own power to establish his own authority. Matthew emphasized that Jesus submitted absolutely to the power and authority of God. His triumph was a revelation of the real power and the authentic authority of God that were given to him as a result of his prayer in Gethsemane: "My Father, if it is possible, let this cup pass from me; yet not what I want but what you want" (26:39). The picture that dominates the scene is not that of an emotionally unsettled person who wanted to punish himself but of a balanced individual who wanted to do the will of God more than he wanted to save his life. The triumph of Jesus in Gethsemane was the triumph of God's mercy in him. His decision to be the instrument of God's mercy meant that he renounced all special privileges in order to fulfill the special responsibility of his vocation. His watching and praying in Gethsemane were the actions that carried out the commitment that he had made at the beginning of his ministry when he was baptized by John (3:13-17).
—The struggle with Satan and with the embodiment of Satan in Peter came to a climax when Jesus died to his own will in Gethsemane (4:1-11; 16:21-23). The Crucifixion made explicit and public what had already been privately decided in the secrecy of his heart.
—The same point may be made about the Resurrection. When Jesus chose to live in dependence upon God, he committed himself to the invincible power and everlasting authority of God. Therefore he was already raised from the dead and triumphant over all his foes, even death itself. The Resurrection simply made explicit and public what had already been privately decided in the secrecy of his heart. The connection between his death and his Resurrection was absolutely essential to understanding his ministry. His death was not the accidental unfolding of a personal tragedy but the ultimate expression of his vocation: to reveal the mercy of God. His Resurrection was not the miraculous resuscitation of a corpse but the ultimate manifestation of the invincible power and everlasting authority of God: God's mercy triumphant.
—Therefore the stories about the Resurrection do not affirm that Jesus rose from the dead but that "he has been raised" (28:6). The Resurrection like all of his ministry was not what he did but what God did in him.

(F) Discuss how the Resurrection reveals the death of Jesus as the power of the universe.

- Begin the discussion by sharing that faith in the Resurrection in general is not the distinctive element of Christian faith. The Resurrection of the *crucified* Jesus is the distinctive element (28:5-6). The death of Jesus was what scandalized his followers as well as his foes. The Resurrection affirms that the event that caused his followers' desertion and that his enemies interpreted as the sign that God also had deserted him was the reason God raised him up and claimed him as God's beloved Son. The Resurrection, then, is the divine reversal of all human values. Instead of Jesus being powerless in death, he is the one who embodies the power of God. Instead of his being stripped of all authority in death, he is endowed with the power of God.
- Return to the same groups of three (if your class is large).
- Invite the class to consider the following questions:
—How does Jesus' prayer in Gethsemane foreshadow his crucifixion?
—How does Jesus' prayer in Gethsemane foreshadow his resurrection?
—How does Jesus' triumph in Gethsemane reverse the assumptions of his friends and his foes?
—Does faith in the Resurrection require us to rethink our understanding of true power and authentic authority?

Dimension 3: What Does the Bible Mean to Us?

(G) Imagine your own Gethsemane.

- Provide art supplies such as those that you have used before (modeling clay, crayon, markers, paper, chalk, paint, glue, and scissors).
- Instruct class members to create images that reflect

crises in their own lives. Suggest that such crises occur in moments when they were compelled to choose between divine things and human things.

Note: It is important that you consider your own crisis events in advance of leading this session. If you are comfortable, share one with the class as one example.

- Again, in small groups if your class is large, reflect on the images in light of your development of this lesson. Guide a discussion by raising the following questions:
—How does Jesus' experience in Gethsemane shed light on our own experiences of Gethsemane?
—What are some of the divine things that we have chosen in our Gethsemanes?
—What are some of the human things that we have chosen in our Gethsemanes because they appeared to be divine things?
—Why must we all go with Jesus to a place called Gethsemane?

Perhaps the most dangerous misuse of this text is to assume that, if we had been confronted with the testing of Peter and the ten other disciples in Gethsemane, we would have not failed as they failed. If we read the text as a report of their failure without allowing it to illuminate our own failures, then it leads to self-righteousness, harsh judgments about others, exclusion of others from our compassion, and illusions about our own strength. Such an interpretation of the text also serves as a barrier to our experiencing the steadfastness of Jesus as the embodiment of God's mercy. If we are ever going to begin our journey from the failure of self-confidence to the triumph of confidence in God, we must acknowledge that our hope rests upon the fact that "God is with us" even when we have failed to "stay awake and pray."

(H) Rewrite Jesus' prayer.

Clearly Matthew intends his readers to experience Jesus' prayer in Gethsemane as the climactic moment in his life and ministry. After he had prayed for the third time, "My Father, if this cannot pass unless I drink it, your will be done" (42), he had already entered into his death and had already been raised to victory over the tomb. We do not learn to pray as he prayed by repeating the words but by taking the journey with him.

- Distribute paper and pencils to class members.
- Post newsprint in the front of the classroom on which has been written the Lord's Prayer (6:9-13) in large letters.
- Recite the Lord's Prayer together.
- Assign class members the task of rewriting Jesus' prayer, without using any of his words. (This will enable class members to reflect on their own experiences of finding strength to keep awake and pray in hours of testing.)
- Provide time for individuals to share their rewrites of the prayer with the entire class.
- If possible, post the prayers in a visible place in the classroom or (if the authors are willing) print them in a handout and distribute to class members next Sunday.

(I) Sing the Lord's Prayer.

- Using the hymnals of your congregation, discover hymns based on the Lord's Prayer.
- Sing several of these hymns OR use a common hymn tune and sing the prayers of your class.
- Share the following information with the class.

—Jesus affirmed throughout the Gospel of Matthew that God is good and can be trusted to give good things to all people (6:25-34; 7:7-11; 19:13-30). One of the signs of God's goodness was that people were given a vocation and the resources necessary for fulfilling their vocation.

—Jesus' vocation was a divine calling that gave his life purpose and meaning. He was able to conform to God's will, to serve rather than to be served. He was able to be merciful to all, because he was filled with the power of God, the Holy Spirit. He called his disciples to participate in his ministry of compassion, and they were equipped by the Spirit to serve as he had served (9:35-10:42; 20:20-23).

—The reward for fulfilling one's vocation was treasure in heaven, "where neither moth nor rust consumes and where thieves do not break in and steal" (6:19-21). In Gethsemane Jesus chose treasure in heaven rather than treasure on earth. The result of his decision was his resurrection. The Resurrection, then, was the confirmation of the quality of his life. Since he valued the goodness of God more than any earthly good and trusted the goodness of God more than any earthly power, those who had power to kill his body had no power to kill his soul.

—There is no doubt that Jesus' triumph was not his alone. It was the triumph that he expected all of his disciples to share with him, because it was possible for them to value God's goodness more than any earthly good and to trust God's goodness more than any earthly power (10:26-31).

—If we want to know the meaning of treasure in heaven, we must fix our attention upon the words and deeds of Jesus. In him we experience God's unconditional mercy that is the ultimate treasure because it is God's very nature and therefore endures forever. When we choose mercy as our ultimate good and make it the object of our deepest longing, then we are transformed by the treasure of our hearts.

—Just as the resurrection of Jesus confirmed the quality of his life, so our resurrection will confirm the quality of our lives. We do not have to wait until the moment of our death to experience the power of the Resurrection, for where our treasure is, there our heart will be also.

(J) Discuss mercy.

- Ask the class to make a list of personal qualities that they admire most in other people.
- Record the list on newsprint or a chalkboard.
- Lead the class in analyzing the list in light of the quality of God's mercy revealed in Jesus.
- Invite groups of three to consider the following questions.
—Do the qualities we admire in others reveal the treasure of our hearts?
—What are the admirable qualities in others that are derived from mercy?
—What do we ordinarily mean when we say that a person is "godly"?
—How do the words and deeds of Jesus help us to treasure mercy with all our heart?
- Share the responses of the small groups in the larger class.

(K) Pray together.

- Invite one or more class members to use the qualities identified in the preceding activity as a kind of closing litany or prayer.
- As each quality is read aloud, invite the class to pray together, "Lord, use your Spirit to make us more merciful."
- Close by praying together the Lord's Prayer.

Additional Bible Helps

Glimpses of Jesus' Vocation
The text affirms Jesus as having a special relationship with God. Jesus quoted a passage from the Hebrew Scripture about the striking of the shepherd that resulted in the scattering of the flock. The identification of Jesus as the shepherd would have been acceptable to first century Christians. Matthew's readers found it difficult, however, to accept that Jesus' role as God's shepherd did not give him protection from harm. It, in fact, exposed him to unusual suffering.

In order for Jesus to fulfill his vocation as shepherd of the flock, he had to give his life for the sheep. Doing so was necessary because God desired mercy rather than sacrifice. Jesus as the merciful shepherd conformed to God's will. He was delivered to sinners. What happened to him at the hands of sinners was not the frustration of God's salvation but the fulfillment. Those who seemed to have the authority and power to resist God and to thwart God's promised salvation were in fact used by God and made agents of God's authority and power.

The situation of tragic suffering, rejection, and death were transformed by Jesus' choice of divine things rather than human things. He read the Scriptures in order to understand God's will for his life and to conform to God's will. He interpreted the Scripture from Zechariah 13:7 to include his enemies and his friends in God's mercy and to confirm his own commitment to a ministry of mercy. He did not seize upon the scattering of his followers as an occasion to condemn them for their failures but to promise them that he would not desert them and would gather them together again after his resurrection. "But after I am raised up, I will go ahead of you to Galilee" (26:32).

Throughout his suffering, rejection, death, and resurrection, Jesus revealed the meaning of becoming like children: "Truly I tell you, unless you change and become like children, you will never enter the kingdom of heaven. Whoever becomes humble like this child is the greatest in the kingdom of heaven" (18:3-4).

Peter and the ten other disciples were unable to accept Jesus' interpretation of Scripture because they had been taught to use Scripture to exclude others and to claim special privilege for themselves. They were still convinced that Jesus' special relationship to God would protect him from all harm. They were also convinced that their special relationship to Jesus would assure them of victory over their foes. Since they rejected Jesus' understanding of his vocation as a call to serve rather than to be served, they rejected his call to serve rather than to be served. Their basic problem was that they had confused human things and divine things. They had set their minds on those things with no enduring value.

The truth about Peter and the ten other disciples was that they trusted themselves rather than God. Mercy was not a possibility for them because they put their trust in themselves. The positive side of their faith was that they trusted their own status and privilege to provide for their needs and to give them the authority and power to protect themselves. The negative side of their faith was that they gave up the security of God's goodness and renounced the authority and power of God. They were not the agents of God's mercy because they neglected their relationship to God by complacently clinging to their own self-sufficiency.

Throughout the narrative of Jesus' suffering, rejection, death, and resurrection, his disciples revealed that because they failed to change and become like children, they also failed to enter the kingdom of heaven. Their preoccupation with their own greatness kept them from the greatness of the Kingdom given freely to all who became humble like a child.

13
Matthew 28:1-20
The Ministry of Jesus the Messiah Continued: Commission and Promise

LEARNING MENU
Drawing on what you know to be most effective with your class, choose at least one activity from Dimensions 1, 2, and 3.

Dimension 1: What Does the Bible Say?

The Gospel of Matthew begins with the report of Jesus' birth and ends with the report of his resurrection. Jesus' life and ministry come to a fitting climax with the report of his triumph over death. Yet the end does not complete the narrative. In this lesson you will discover the following:
—The Gospel of Matthew takes up the themes of the beginning and enlarges and expands them so that the end is another beginning.
—Jesus' life and ministry is continued and fulfilled in the ministry of his disciples.
—The ministry of Jesus' disciples is continued and fulfilled in the life and ministry of the disciples of all nations.
—Jesus himself is an essential part of the unfolding history as the disciples remember his promise: "I am with you always, to the end of the age."

(A) Answer the questions in the study book.

Spend a few moments reviewing students' answers to the questions in the study book, pages 100-101. (Allow additional time for students who have not done so to answer the questions. Another method would be to assign small groups of three students to discuss the answers together, without taking time for class members to write down their reflections.)
Possible answers to these questions include

1. Earthquakes are traditional apocalyptic symbols. Here it indicates that the Resurrection is an end-time event. That the stone is rolled away by an angel merely reminds us that the Resurrection is of God, who does things human beings cannot.

2. The reactions of the women are human reactions. How would you have reacted to such news?

3. The charge about the stolen body was used to counteract the effect the Resurrection may have had.

4. The Great Commission commands the church to enter into the Gentile mission. It is a fitting conclusion and effective summary of the Gospel.

5. The promise of the continuing presence of Christ is the equal to the promise given in Matthew 1:23—the Emmanuel promise.

(B) Compare the birth and Resurrection stories.

- Select members of the class to play the necessary roles in each of the stories.
- Dramatize the birth narrative as Matthew recorded it in 1:18-25.
- Follow with the dramatization of the Resurrection events recorded in Matthew 28.
- In groups of three, reflect on what has been seen and heard. Consider using the following questions:
— Who were the principal characters in the stories?
— Who seemed to do the work of God? Who did not?
— What points of similarities or comparison can you discover in the two stories?
— If you had been present at either the birth or resurrection of Jesus what might your response have been?
- Points of similarity and contrast in the two stories should be noted on chalkboard or newsprint, as small groups report the highlights of their discussions to the large group.

The following are some of the points of **similarity**:
— God is the primary actor in both stories.
— The Holy Spirit is emphasized in both stories.
— An angel of the Lord reveals the action of God in both stories.
— Attention is focused on Jesus in both stories.
— In both stories the action of God is fulfilled by the obedience of humans.
— In both stories God's action includes women as essential actors in the accomplishment of God's purpose.

The following are some of the points of **contrast**:
— The angel of the Lord appears to Joseph in a dream.
— Mary, the mother of Jesus, is in the background and plays no active part.
— Mary Magdalene and the other Mary are principal actors.
— The women are addressed directly by the angel of the Lord and obey the angel's commands.
— Mary Magdalene and the other Mary are the first to hear the message of the Resurrection and the first to carry the message to others.
— The women are the first to experience the risen Lord and to be commissioned by him.
— The enemies of Jesus have a prominent role in the Resurrection. Their attempt to deny the Resurrection is reminiscent of Herod's attempt to kill the infant Jesus.
— The story of the Resurrection includes Jesus' disciples in his vocation and uses them to accomplish the salvation of the Gentiles.
— The mission to the Gentiles is to be accomplished by baptism "in the name of the Father and of the Son and of the Holy Spirit" and by "teaching them to obey everything that I have commanded you."
— The birth story seems to focus exclusively on the descendants of Abraham, but the Resurrection story reaches out inclusively to "all nations."

The class will probably identify other points of similarity and contrast that will illustrate the connection between the beginning and the end of Matthew's witness to the life and ministry of Jesus.

(C) Debrief after the comparison experience.

The task of finding differences or similarities in the birth and Resurrection stories may have been stimulating. Spend a few moments applying your findings to our lives today.

- Again using the same groups of three, and assigning each group one of the questions from below, discuss
— The angel of the Lord appears in both narratives to tell how God has acted and how people are to respond to God's action. What is the meaning of an angel of the Lord? How do we appropriate this meaning for our own lives?
— What does the prominent role of Mary Magdalene and the other Mary in the Resurrection story suggest about the status and role of women in Matthew's community? Are there implications for the status and role of women in today's church?
— The birth story states clearly that Jesus' vocation is to "save his people from their sins." How can you account for the inclusion of "all nations" in the vocation that he gave to his disciples? What implications does this have for us?

Dimension 2: What Does the Bible Mean?

(D) Compare experiences at Gethsemane and the tomb.

- Invite a class member to read aloud Matthew 26:36-46 and another member to read aloud 28:1-10.
- Lead the class in a period of reflection by raising the following issues:
— What is the connection between Jesus' commitment to the will of God and his resurrection?
— Does the text support the conclusion that Jesus' acceptance of the will of God was a choice to die to himself and to live to God?
— Does the pattern of Jesus' obedience, followed by his resurrection, suggest the pattern of the obedience of the women at the tomb followed by their experience of the Resurrection?

—Did the women at the tomb choose to die to self and live to God when they heard and obeyed the angel of the Lord?

—Is the obedience of the women their witness to the Resurrection?

(E) Create artistic images.

- Ask class members to imagine how they would have acted if they had been guards at the tomb or chief priests and elders.
- Have available drawing materials (such as paper, newsprint, pencils, markers, or crayons) and modeling clay.
- Invite class members to prepare (draw, mold, or write) an interpretation of what happened at the tomb from the viewpoint of the guards, chief priests, and elders.
- Conclude the exercise by giving class members the opportunity to share their images or written descriptions with the entire class.

(F) Discuss what it means to confess faith in the resurrection of Jesus.

- Provide copies of the Apostles' Creed for all members of the class. You will find it in many Protestant hymnals.
- Recite or read the Creed in unison.
- Call attention to the affirmation of Jesus' resurrection: "On the third day he rose again; he ascended into heaven, is seated at the right hand of the Father, and will come again to judge the living and the dead."
- Distribute paper and pencils.
- Ask each member of the class to write what this affirmation means personally.
- In groups of three, invite class members to share with one another their personal statements.
- Lead the class in discussing how this article of faith is dependent upon Matthew's witness to the Resurrection.

Dimension 3: What Does the Bible Mean to Us?

The situation in the contemporary church is not radically different from the situation which Matthew addressed in the church at Antioch. At an intellectual level, most people who are members of the Christian community today affirm the resurrection of Jesus as true. Our problem with the Resurrection, then, is not theoretical but practical. We profess with our lips that Jesus has been raised from the dead; we live as if his resurrection has not occurred.

Your task as teacher of this lesson is not to convince the class of new truth about the Resurrection. It is to help the class appropriate the old truth so that faith in the Resurrection will result in leaving the old age of violence and death to enter and serve the new age of mercy and life.

One of the best ways to begin to experience the revolutionary power of the Resurrection is to remember that disappointment, failure, and despair are often the result of following Jesus and providing for him. Mary Magdalene and the other Mary were not spared the experience of the passion of Jesus by becoming his disciples. As he had taught them consistently their participation in his ministry exposed them to the same testing that he encountered. The message that they heard from the angel of the Lord at the tomb was the same message that Jesus had given them about his rejection, suffering, death, and Resurrection on the way from Galilee to Jerusalem (16:21-23; 17:22-23; 20:17-19).

At the tomb his word was confirmed by the word of the angel, which may mean that they experienced what he had already told them. There is no way that we can comprehend exactly what happened. One thing is certain. The women "left the tomb quickly with fear and great joy, and ran to tell his disciples" (28:8).

The lessons we can learn from this seem to be clear:

—We do not enter the new age of mercy and life by arguing about our theories of the Resurrection.

—How Jesus was raised from the dead is none of our business and to speculate about it is to wander off into the blind alley of idle discussion.

—Our task is to follow Jesus as Mary Magdalene and the other Mary followed Jesus all the way to the tomb.

—Just as Jesus did not come to victory over death except by way of the cross, so we will not come to the experience of the Resurrection except by way of the cross. If we really want to experience the angel of the Lord and see the stone rolled away and feel the earth shake under us, then we must obey the plain teaching of Jesus to all his disciples, "If any want to become my followers, let them deny themselves and take up their cross and follow me" (16:24). The gate to the new age is the tomb, and the road to the new age is the way of the cross. "For the gate is narrow and the road is hard that leads to life, and there are few who find it" (7:14).

(G) Experience the difference between our celebration of Easter and Matthew's witness to the Resurrection.

- Invite the class to sit quietly and think of those things in our culture that are associated with the celebration of Easter.
- In "popcorn fashion" (sharing responses as quickly as possible), list the results on a chalkboard or newsprint.
- Ask the class to reflect on Matthew's witness to the

Resurrection by concentrating on the experience of Mary Magdalene and the other Mary.
- List the results on a chalkboard or newsprint.
- Lead the class to identify points of contrast and similarity between the two lists.
- Focus the discussion by raising the following questions:
—In what ways has the church been influenced more by our cultural celebration of Easter than by Matthew's witness to the Resurrection?
—To what extent might we have actually denied the Resurrection while seeming to celebrate Easter?

(H) Discuss how the risen Lord calls us to service.

- Form groups of three.
- Assign to each group the task of discussing how Jesus comes to us as the risen Lord in the form of the hungry, the thirsty, the stranger, the sick, and the prisoner.
- Ask each group to discuss how we recognize the authority of Jesus when we show mercy to the least of these members of his family.
- Conclude the exercise by asking each group to share experiences that confirm that Jesus' promise to be with us always has been fulfilled in our lives.
- Invite small groups to share highlights of their discussion with the entire class.

(I) Sing about the Resurrection.

- Using your congregation's hymnal, look up and sing several hymns about the Resurrection.
- Consider the following questions:
—What symbols are used in the hymn to speak of the Resurrection?
—What do you feel as you sing these hymns?
- If time allows, break into small groups to write additional verses to familiar Easter hymn tunes.
- Sing your verses as you close this session or as you gather again next Sunday. Note: You may want to choose between this activity and the next activity (J) instead of trying to do both.

(J) Write cinquain poems.

- Distribute paper and pencils; then invite class members to write cinquain poems (poems that have five brief lines) reflecting on images they have received from this study of Matthew.
- Instructions for writing cinquains are
—Line 1: Title (one word; a noun)
—Line 2: Describes the title (two words)
—Line 3: Action words or a phrase about the title (three words; at least one verb)
—Line 4: Describes a feeling about the title (four words)
—Line 5: A word renaming the title or meaning the same thing as the title (one word; a noun)
The following is an example of a cinquain:
God
great creator
acting for persons
always willing to forgive
love

Additional Bible Helps

Matthew's Gospel for the Christians of Antioch

Since Matthew was writing primarily for the Christian community at Antioch, he assumed that his audience already accepted the report of Jesus' resurrection as true. The problem was that many of the followers of Jesus still acted as if the Resurrection had not occurred. Theoretically the Resurrection was affirmed but practically it was denied. Consequently, Matthew did not try to convince his readers that the Resurrection had occurred. Rather he concentrated upon helping them to realize how the event had inaugurated a new age. He also told them how they could enter into the new age by continuing the ministry of Jesus the Messiah.

According to Matthew no one saw Jesus raised from the dead and released from the tomb. Apparently Mary Magdalene, the other Mary, and the guards at the tomb all saw the same supernatural events: the angel of the Lord, the stone rolled back, the angel seated on the stone, and a great earthquake. The guards were overwhelmed by fear and became like dead men.

The difference between the guards and the women was that the women "had followed Jesus from Galilee and had provided for him." They had not fled when he was crucified but "were also there, looking on from a distance" (55). They came to the tomb as followers of Jesus and were delivered by the angel from the fear of the awful events that occurred. They were looking for Jesus who was crucified. The word of the angel told them what had happened. The crucified Jesus had been raised. The tomb had no power to hold him.

The women were commissioned by the angel to carry the same message to the scattered disciples. They were also to announce that the message of the Resurrection would be confirmed by their experience of the Resurrection in Galilee.

The women's response was to obey the message of the angel. They left the tomb before they had any experience of the Resurrection. They believed the word in spite of the fact that it filled them with fear of the mystery of God's intervention in their lives. Their fear was coupled with joy because the message of the angel told them that the love of Jesus that had drawn them to him did not end at the cross but continued to lead them into the new age of mercy and life.

They left the tomb and ran to tell the disciples what they had heard. On the way they were met by Jesus who greeted them and revealed himself to them.

They were the first to experience the risen Lord, for they had become like little children in his service. They were examples of greatness in the kingdom of heaven because they humbled themselves, "took hold of his feet, and worshiped him" (28:9).

The message of the angel was confirmed in them by their experience of the Resurrection and by the vocation that they received from their risen Lord: "Do not be afraid; go and tell my brothers to go to Galilee; there they will see me" (28:10).

The experience of the Resurrection was possible because the message was delivered by God's messenger (the angel) and obeyed by God's servants (Mary Magdalene and the other Mary). Since they heard the word of the Resurrection and obeyed it, they left the old age of violence and death (the tomb) and entered the new age of mercy and life (the service of the risen Lord). The implications for the church at Antioch were clear.

They received the message of the Resurrection just as the women received it. The message would become meaningful for them as it delivered them from fear and as they obeyed it by becoming as little children in the service of the Risen One.

A sign that they had heard the message was their joy as they left the old age of violence and death and followed Jesus on the way of mercy and life. The only way that they could be with him in the new age was to join with him in the work of the new age, the work of reconciliation in the family of the God of mercy.

The Resurrection, then, was not just what they said but what they were called to do in the service of the crucified who had been raised from the dead. "Not everyone who says to me, 'Lord, Lord,' will enter the kingdom of heaven, but only the one who does the will of my Father in heaven" (7:21).

How to Create Excitement for Bible Study

by Debra and Gary Ball-Kilbourne

Acts 8:26-40 tells the story of Philip and the Ethiopian eunuch. The eunuch was reading the words of the prophet Isaiah while riding in a chariot. Philip approached him and asked, " 'Do you understand what you are reading?' He replied, 'How can I, unless someone guides me?' And he invited Philip to get in and sit beside him" (Acts 8:30-31).

Philip may not have realized it, but he was teaching a one-person Bible class at that point. How effective was Philip as a teacher? The Bible tells us that the Ethiopian became so excited by what he was taught that he asked to be baptized on the spot.

How can we instill even a fraction of that kind of excitement in the Bible classes we teach?

Too many adult Bible classes follow the same pattern Sunday after Sunday. Standing in front of the class members, the teacher lectures on the Bible text for that week. Attempts at discussion fall flat. The class members continue to attend, perhaps out of a sense of obligation, loyalty, or the need for fellowship. But are they truly being fed from the rich feast of the Scriptures?

What can be done to spice up such an adult Bible class? Three steps can lead your class members into a freshly exciting encounter with God through the words of the Bible: 1) Do your homework. 2) Share your excitement. 3) Risk leading your class members into creativity.

Do Your Homework.

No substitute exists for solid preparation of the material you will teach. To do your homework means to spend time studying the material and developing your lesson before Saturday night.

Take the time to read through the material. Read the Bible text several times. If you usually read the New Revised Standard Version of the Bible, read two or more additional versions. *The Jerusalem Bible, The New English Bible,* and the *Good News Bible* would be good choices. Reading these can help you see the different variations in meaning given to the text by translators. Make notes of points or words about which you have questions or that you think are significant.

Consider the following questions:
1. Who wrote the text?
2. When and where was it written?
3. For what audience was it written?
4. Why was it written?
5. What points of contact do your class members have with the situations and needs of the persons who first heard or read the Bible passage you are studying?

Doing your homework will be hard work at times. But it will enrich you *and* the people you teach. Two excellent resources for helping you learn how to study the Bible are *Get Acquainted With Your Bible*, by Gary L. Ball-Kilbourne (Abingdon, 1993), or *Church Bible Study Handbook*, by Robin Maas (Abingdon, 1982).

Share Your Excitement.

If you act bored or indifferent, your class members will too. Suppose you go looking for a new car at a local automobile dealership. The salesperson seems uninterested in selling a car to you. He or she mumbles a few of the facts and figures about the model, shrugs his or her shoulders at your questions, yawns, and looks pointedly at the clock.

Would you really want to buy a car from a salesperson who is not excited about it?

In much the same way you will have a difficult time getting your class members excited about studying the Bible if you are not excited about it. Indeed, if excitement about the good news of Jesus had not crept into Philip's explanation of the Scriptures, the Holy Spirit would probably have found it quite difficult to convert the Ethiopian.

Be enthusiastic as you teach. Let your class members see in your own spirit how God's Spirit filled you with life when you studied the Bible text. Tell them about the struggles you may have had in attempting to understand the difficult parts. Celebrate new insights. Move around. Get excited!

Risk Leading Your Class Members Into Creativity. The McDonald's Corporation established an innovative policy several years ago in an attempt to foster creativity in its executives. Top managers of the corporation were encouraged to spend some time each week looking through a skylight in the ceiling while resting on a waterbed in a quiet setting. The reason? Meditation in such a setting led McDonald's executives to dream up creative, fresh, and potentially rewarding marketing techniques. McDonald's profitable decision to serve breakfast was, in part, a result of this "waterbed" policy.

When was the last time you spent quality time reflecting about the class you lead and dreaming about how it might be improved?

One important goal of teaching is to help class members convert the material taught into knowledge they can apply to their daily lives. The lecture method is less effective in doing this than other approaches that require greater participation by the class members. Yet, many teachers continue to lecture week after week for fear of trying new teaching methods.

The Adult Bible Class of Riverdale Community Church was studying the Nativity stories one Advent. As teachers of the class, we had done our homework. We had gained several new insights into the Bible texts, especially through reading Raymond E. Brown's *The Birth of the Messiah: A Commentary on the Infancy Narratives of Matthew and Luke* (Doubleday, 1993). We were excited about what we had learned. But how could we share our excitement and knowledge with the class members?

Taking a deep breath, we decided to try an innovative approach. At several locations in the classroom we arranged chairs in a circle. We called each of these circles a "learning center." We then divided the class members into small groups of persons and asked each group to move to a learning center to carry out a specific assignment.

At one learning center we asked persons to read Matthew 2 and Luke 1:5—2:20 and note the differences and similarities in these two accounts of Jesus' birth. In another center we asked the class members to examine the ways familiar Christmas carols celebrate the Nativity and refer to Jesus. In the third learning center we invited class members to create birth announcement cards that would express their feelings about Jesus' birth. Persons in the fourth center studied basic information about shepherds in first-century Judea. We asked these class members to think about what it would have been like to be a shepherd in those days. How would it have felt to be despised throughout Jewish society and yet be among the first to hear the good news of Jesus' birth?

Toward the end of the session we came together as a whole class and shared our new learnings with one another. People were bubbling over with excitement about what they had discovered. They had truly found themselves involved, as if for the first time, with the old, familiar well-loved story of Jesus' birth. Some class members had never been aware of the differences between Luke's and Matthew's accounts of the Nativity. Few of the class members had ever tried to put themselves in the shepherds' place. Most persons appreciated the opportunity to express their learnings and feelings in the birth announcement cards they made.

Creative teaching methods abound if you are willing to learn them and risk using them. You might want to try such different and creative ways of involving class members in the Bible text as

1. dramatic readings;
2. poetry writing;
3. map study;
4. word study using concordances and/or Bible dictionaries;
5. art displays depicting a biblical story or character from various points of view.

In some classes members are accustomed to sitting rigidly in straight lines of chairs or pews. Every week the leader attempts to pour information into the class members' minds like water flowing from a faucet into a bucket. In these classes something as simple as asking members to discuss a question in groups of three may create excitement and interest. Perhaps you might want to invite a neighboring church's adult class to study with you one quarter. Doing so might be particularly challenging if the other church is made up primarily of persons with a different ethnic or racial background than yours. The ideas are almost limitless. Spend some "waterbed time" dreaming up exciting, fresh leadership techniques for use with your class.

For further ideas on creative methods to use and adapt, try *Teaching the Bible to Adults and Youth*, by Dick Murray (Abingdon, 1993).

Adapted from "How to Create Excitement for Bible Study," by Debra and Gary Ball-Kilbourne; *Adult Bible Studies Teaching Helps*, SON 1986. Copyright ©1986 by Graded Press.

Matthew and His Gospel

By James R. Woodward

This article tells the story of a businessman Jesus called from his place of business so he would become prepared to write the "Greatest Story Ever Told." A great many of the pieces of the story of Matthew's life are lost to history. As a result, one must improvise at times. My purpose is to suggest an easily remembered narrative that explains the major facets of Matthew's Gospel in order to make your teaching more successful.

After reading through many introductions to Matthew's Gospel in various commentaries, I was left with the impression that nobody knows who Matthew really was. No one knows for sure where he wrote his Gospel or what his purpose was. Then I discovered that Edgar Goodspeed wrote a marvelous book titled *Matthew, Apostle and Evangelist* (The John C. Winston Company, 1959; out of print). In this book Goodspeed reasons out the background of and purpose for Matthew's Gospel. Since my hope in writing this article is to help you better understand Matthew and his Gospel, I would like to share Goodspeed's interpretation with you.

Matthew's Call
"Therefore every scribe who has been trained for the kingdom of heaven is like the master of a householder who brings out of his treasure what is new and what is old" (Matthew 13:52). This verse of Scripture may be a summary of Matthew's background at the time he became a follower of Jesus.

The abrupt call of Matthew (also known as Levi) recorded in Mark 2:14 is unusual because it is the only specific instance of a single disciple being called. Could Jesus have had a specific work in mind for Matthew? Jesus called the four fishermen to be fishers of men (Mark 1:16-20). Could he have called Matthew to be the scribe for men?

Matthew's father, Alphaeus (Mark 2:14), had apparently sent Matthew to scribal school. Matthew used his training daily in keeping the tax ledgers. Tax collectors were not paid a salary but usually bought their office. Under such circumstances Matthew could leave his post as tax collector without Rome arresting him for desertion.

Jesus seems to have found Matthew's whole family predisposed toward his movement. Another son of Alphaeus, James the less, later became Jesus' disciple (Matthew 10:3). Mark mentions still another brother, Joses, who was probably also a follower of Jesus (Mark 15:40, 47).

Matthew's mother, Mary, was a witness to both the Crucifixion and the Resurrection (Matthew 27:56; 28:1-10). She may have been the one to tell Matthew some of the details of the Crucifixion and Resurrection events. Since the Scriptures refer to her as the mother of James and Joses but not of Matthew, Mary may have been Matthew's stepmother.

We hear little of the father, Alphaeus, as a person; but the Bible calls attention to him as the father of these three sons and the husband of Mary. If he had not been well known in Christian circles, his name would not have been used as a means of identification.

Matthew, the scribe turned tax collector, probably became a personal secretary to Jesus in the same way that Baruch was to the prophet Jeremiah (Jeremiah 36:4). Baruch copied down everything Jeremiah said and published his works after Jeremiah's death. I believe Jesus chose Matthew to insure that his words would be saved for the future. Matthew's training and tax collector's experience uniquely equipped him for his new calling.

Matthew probably was in the habit of taking Jesus' words down in Aramaic (the part-Persian-part-Hebrew-language acquired while the people of Israel were in Babylonian captivity) and then translating them into the Greek of that day. Papias, an early Christian bishop, wrote in A.D. 140 of Matthew's "teachings of Jesus" in Aramaic. This material was probably a copy of Matthew's scribal notes of Jesus' teachings that Matthew later combined with Mark's Gospel to make the Gospel of Matthew. Perhaps the reason the Gospels have little information about Matthew is that he was busy collecting Jesus' teachings on tax collectors' scrolls that his friends in the business furnished.

Matthew's Ministry

After the resurrection of Jesus and his commission to his disciples to go into all the world, Matthew apparently began to look around for a place to use his talents. What better place than the missionary-minded church at Antioch? This church was not only interracial but international in thought and deeds.

Do you remember how the Antioch church began? Some Christians from Cyprus and Cyrene started an interracial church of Jews and Gentiles. The Jerusalem church sent Barnabas, a native of Cyprus, to Antioch to see what was happening. He was so excited by the success of the new church that he went to Tarsus for Paul (known then as Saul). They worked in Antioch for some time before they began their first missionary journey (Acts 11:19—13:3).

The leaders of this church had various backgrounds. Barnabas was a Jew of priestly heritage. Paul was a Jew trained as a Pharisee. Simeon was a black man. Lucius was an Arab from Cyrene (which was Tripoli or present-day Libya). Manean, former friend of Herod, was probably a one-time Roman soldier as well. No wonder Matthew the Levite turned tax collector turned Christian fit in! Here in this church he could quietly teach in Greek and Aramaic while awaiting the second coming of his Lord.

In the beginning Christians formed prayer groups within the formal structure of Judaism, much the same way the Methodist Societies were prayer groups within the Anglican Church. (Only later was Christianity separated from its Jewish heritage and then persecuted.) When the great Jewish four-year war broke out in Jerusalem in A.D. 66, Christians fled the hills, swelling the ranks of the Antioch church.

Antioch exists even today as a small town about two hundred miles due north of Damascus, on the border of Turkey. In the first century the city was third largest in the Roman Empire and quite cosmopolitan. Matthew probably was teaching there when he received news of the torture and death of his old friend Simon Peter and of Mark's Gospel, the first Christian book written in Greek.

Peter had preached his experiences in the presence of his assistant, John Mark. Mark had also heard parts of the life of Jesus and Jesus' teachings that Peter used as sermon illustrations. When Peter was martyred, Mark wrote what he remembered as a way of preserving Peter's message.

Meanwhile, Matthew, who expected Jesus to return at any time, was in his place in Antioch patiently teaching. He probably had had no thought of writing a book. Then Matthew read Mark's Gospel and said, in effect, "I've got to tell the world how the life of Jesus began and that it never really ended." Matthew knew the time was short. He must publish all he recalled of Jesus' teachings as well as arrange the events mentioned in Mark's Gospel in the sequence he had experienced.

Thus, Matthew must have transcribed all his notes from Aramaic into Greek and then called some other Christians to gather around him for the job of copying. As this Christian teacher pronounced the words of Jesus, the faithful Christians published what one reviewer, eighteen hundred years later, called the "Greatest Work Ever Written."

As long as Christianity was part of Judaism, there was no need for Matthew's Gospel. After the fall of Jerusalem, Matthew's Gospel helped Jewish Christians find an easy transition from Judaism to an interracial, international church.

How Is Matthew's Gospel Organized

The first five books of the Old Testament were originally one scroll of continuous narrative describing events from Creation and the Fall to redemption in the Promised Land. The portions of these books that describe the life of Moses alternate between the narrative and the teachings of Moses. Matthew's Gospel uses a similar alternating pattern to protray Jesus as one greater then Moses.

Some scholars divide the book of Matthew one way and some another. The following is my suggestion for dividing the book. The similarities to the outline of the life of Moses are striking.

The prologue (Matthew 1—4) includes the birth story with a ruler who tries to kill off all male Hebrews under two years of age. Then comes the escape to Egypt and later return to Nazareth. In a similar manner Moses as an infant was in danger of losing his life at the hands of the secular authorities but managed to escape death. Moses also fled to another country for a period of time and returned home at God's command.

Chapters 3—25 deal with Jesus' ministry. Notice the balance Matthew maintains between the story of Jesus' life and the account of his teachings, just as is true of the Scripture about Moses. The balance between Jesus' action and his sayings is as follows: first story (3—4) and teachings (5—7) (I believe Matthew put the Sermon on the Mount in the front of his Gospel so all his readers could see that one greater than Moses has brought a greater law of the Spirit down from the new mountain.); second story (8:1—10:4) and teachings (10:5—11:1); third story (11:2—12:50) and teachings (13:1-52); fourth story (13:53—17:27) and teachings (18:1—19:2); fifth story (19:3—23:39) and teachings (24—25).

Then comes the conclusion, covering Jesus' death on

Mount Calvary (26—28) being like Moses' death on Mount Pisgah. Just as Moses commissioned Joshua and pointed him toward the Promised Land, so the Great Commission (Matthew 28:16-20) points Jesus' followers toward the nations.

What Is Unique About Matthew's Gospel?

1. The Gospel of Matthew contains many quotations of and references to the Psalms and the books of Isaiah and Jeremiah. Early Christian writings leaned heavily on the passion (suffering and death) of Jesus as the new sacrificial lamb. Matthew gives special stress to Isaiah's and Jeremiah's prophecies because they are grounded in the Old Testament sacrificial system but at the same time emphasize that a new and greater development is about to break forth with a new heaven and new earth (Isaiah 65:17; 66:22). A new type of law and sacrifice planted in the heart will replace the burnt offerings of the old system (Jeremiah 31:31-34). Many of the Psalms contain the personal experiences of those who had a foretaste of these coming events.

2. Matthew has a genealogy that no other Gospel has. Luke 3:23-38 works back from Joseph to Adam. Matthew begins with Abraham and moves through the generations to the birth of the King who is worshiped by kings (the wise men) from the East.

3. Another unique feature of Matthew's Gospel is that it includes the only accounts of the parable of the laborers in the vineyard (20:1-16), the parable of the ten bridesmaids (25:1-13), and the parable of the judgment of the nations (25:31-46). Matthew may have included this material because he wanted to stress watchfulness. He probably realized that a day of accounting for one's actions is part of life.

4. Matthew had a way with figures. Because he was at home in the world of finance, his records of many parables contain references to large sums of money. In the parable of the unforgiving servant (18:23-35), Matthew mentions ten thousand talents, which is something like ten million dollars.

The word *talent* occurs fourteen times in Matthew but never in the other Gospels. Instead of *talent*, Luke used *mina* (translated "pound"), a coin worth about twenty dollars. Luke reported that each man in the parable of the talents had the same amount of money (19:11-27). Contrast Matthew 25:14-30 to see how Matthew dealt with high finances on a graduated scale.

5. Matthew's Gospel employs over one hundred words found nowhere else in the New Testament. Matthew, the businessman, apparently had a much better vocabulary than most of the other writers of the New Testament.

Other Contributions of the Gospel of Matthew

In the Sermon on the Mount we find not only the norms but the demands Jesus placed on the Christian community. Kinds of prayer such as ostentatious prayer (6:5-6), repetitious prayer (6:7-8), and a model prayer (6:9-13) are included.

We can also examine the cost of following Jesus (8:18-22), the characteristics of discipleship (10:32-39; 16:24-28), and calls for watchfulness as disciples (chapters 24—25). The necessity for repeated forgiveness is stressed as well (18:21-35).

For a focus on commitment you may compare the two ways (7:13-14), two trees (7:17-20), two claims (7:21-23), and two builders (7:24-27). Other parables give glimpses of what the Kingdom is like (13:1-52).

Matthew's presentation of the Resurrection and the Great Commission (chapter 28) are still driving forces for followers of the Master.

Adapted from "Matthew and His Gospel," by James R. Woodward; *Adult Bible Studies Teaching Helps*, DJF 1987-88. Copyright ©1987 by Graded Press.

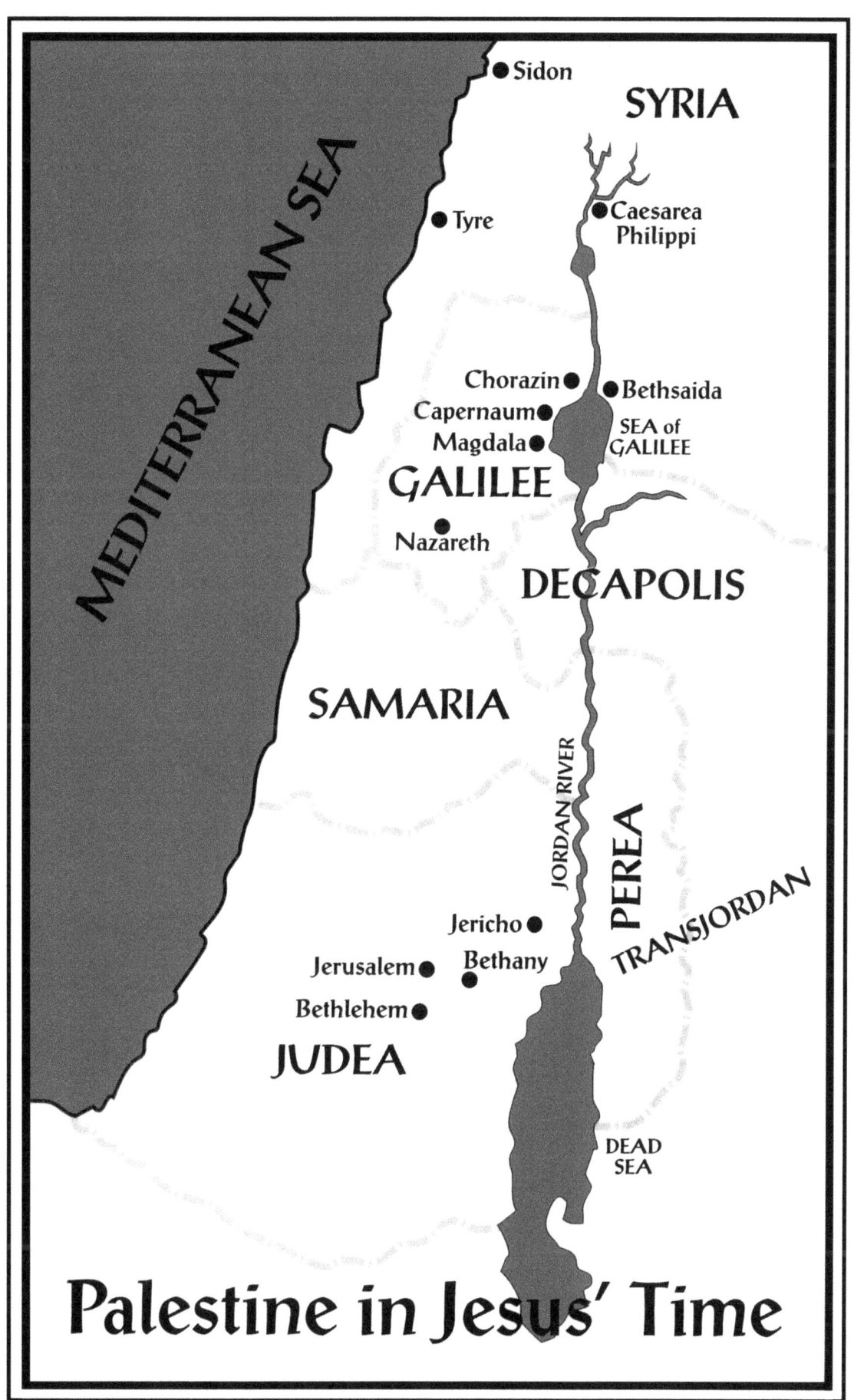

www.ingramcontent.com/pod-product-compliance
Lightning Source LLC
LaVergne TN
LVHW061315060426
835507LV00019B/2170

Copyright © 2011 XAMonline, Inc.
All rights reserved. No part of the material protected by this copyright notice may be reproduced or utilized in any form or by any means, electronic or mechanical, including photocopying, recording or by any information storage and retrievable system, without written permission from the copyright holder.

To obtain permission(s) to use the material from this work for any purpose including workshops or seminars, please submit a written request to:

XAMonline, Inc.
25 First Street, Suite 106
Cambridge, MA 02141
Toll Free: 1-800-509-4128
Email: info@xamonline.com
Web: www.xamonline.com
Fax: 1-617-583-5552

Library of Congress Cataloging-in-Publication Data

Wynne, Sharon A.
    CTEL California Teachers of English Learners Practice Test 1: Teacher Certification / Sharon A. Wynne. -1st ed.
    ISBN: 978-1-60787-317-4
    1. CTEL California Teachers of English Learners Practice Test 1   2. Study Guides
    3. CTEL   4. Teachers' Certification & Licensure   5. Careers

Disclaimer:
The opinions expressed in this publication are the sole works of XAMonline and were created independently from the National Education Association, Educational Testing Service, or any State Department of Education, National Evaluation Systems or other testing affiliates.

Between the time of publication and printing, state specific standards as well as testing formats and website information may change that is not included in part or in whole within this product. Sample test questions are developed by XAMonline and reflect similar content as on real tests; however, they are not former tests. XAMonline assembles content that aligns with state standards but makes no claims nor guarantees teacher candidates a passing score. Numerical scores are determined by testing companies such as NES or ETS and then are compared with individual state standards. A passing score varies from state to state.

Printed in the United States of America   œ-1
CTEL California Teachers of English Learners Practice Test 1
ISBN: 978-1-60787-317-4